HEALTHCARE MARKETING PLANS
that work

David Marlowe

This publication is designed to provide accurate and authoritative information in regard to the subject matter covered. It is sold with the understanding that neither the author nor the publisher is engaged in rendering legal, accounting, or other professional service. If legal advice or other expert assistance is required, the services of a competent professional should be sought.

The views expressed in this publication are strictly those of the author and do not necessarily represent official positions of the Society for Healthcare Strategy and Market Development or the American Hospital Association.

©1999 by David Marlowe. All rights reserved. No part of this publication may be reproduced, stored in a retrieval system, or transmitted, in any form or by any means, electronic, mechanical, photocopying, recording or otherwise, without the prior written permission of the Society for Healthcare Strategy and Market Development. Printed in the United States of America.

ISBN 0-9676441-0-0

Discounts on bulk quantities are available to professional associations, special marketers, educators, trainers and others. For details or to place an order, call 1-800-242-2626 or visit www.ahaonlinestore.com.

About The Author

David Marlowe is a principal with Strategic Marketing Concepts, a healthcare and service industry marketing consulting firm based in Ellicott City, Maryland. In this capacity, Mr. Marlowe directs engagements involving the development of strategic marketing plans, market research, managed care marketing, program development and target audience advertising.

Prior to founding Strategic Marketing Concepts, Mr. Marlowe served as vice president of strategic consulting for First Strategic Group (Whittier, CA), vice president of strategic services for Market Strategies, Inc. (Richmond, VA), vice president of planning and marketing for St. Agnes Hospital (Baltimore, MD), and director of marketing for Harbor Health System (Baltimore, MD). In these positions, Mr. Marlowe has developed over 150 marketing plans for entities ranging from single specialty medical groups to regional managed care plans.

Mr. Marlowe has over 20 years of healthcare marketing and planning experience as a consultant and a provider-based executive. In addition, he has held adjunct faculty positions at Avila College (Kansas City) and the University of Baltimore. Mr. Marlowe is a frequent author and lecturer for national and local professional organizations such as the Alliance for Healthcare Strategy and Marketing, the American College of Healthcare Executives, the Federated Ambulatory Surgery Association, the Medical Group Management Association and the Society for Healthcare Strategy and Market Development. He is the co-author and editor of the book *Building a Foundation for Effective Health Care Market Research* and is on the editorial review boards of *Marketing Health Services* and *Trendwatch*.

Mr. Marlowe holds a bachelor's degree in accounting from Syracuse University and a master of management degree in marketing from the J.L. Kellogg Graduate School of Management at Northwestern University.

Contents

Section	Page
About the Author	v
Acknowledgements	vii
Introduction	1
Case Descriptions	5
Summary of a Marketing Plan Format	9
The Marketing Plan Process	11
The Market Audit	23
Defining a Market Position	43
Determining Market Strategies	49
Setting Quantifiable Market Objectives	55
Defining Market Actions	61
Implementation and Monitoring	91
Conclusion	95
Appendix A – Examples of Background Data	97
Appendix B – Interview Guide Content	101
Appendix C – The Marketing Activity Grid	107
Appendix D – List of Acronyms	115

Acknowledgements

My thanks go to the staff of the Society for Healthcare Strategy and Market Development for their willingness to support this effort and their patience as I dragged the process out until close to retirement age. My special thanks goes to Lauren Barnett for acting as the project champion with the Society's leadership and to Karen Thomas for acting as my conscience. Without Karen's ongoing "nudging" I would have continued to allow small things like work, family and vacations to get in the way of completing the book. Thanks also go to the Board of the Society for allowing this book to go forward and to my many friends and colleagues within the organization who offered encouragement.

My thanks also go to four individuals I have worked with and for over the years—Frank Zilm, Tom Cranshaw, Susan Dubuque and Terri Langhans. All four were great colleagues and mentors. They each had the gift of allowing me to run with my ideas and abilities, while at the same time knowing when to gracefully pull me back from the precipice when I went astray.

I also want to thank the dozens and dozens of organizations that have used my services over the years for the development of marketing plans. Some of these efforts were more successful than others, but the process and output have improved with each plan. The real credit for the content of this book belongs to those organizations that took this process to heart, incorporated it into their marketing "culture" and often took the results to levels that I did not anticipate when we first got started.

Finally, I want to thank my wife Cathy and my son Daniel who showed great tolerance as they shoved food and clean clothes under the door to the den!

Introduction

This is not a book about the myriad issues of marketing health services. We won't be discussing the use of medical call centers to support open enrollment campaigns or the marketing motivations of per diem managed care contracts or the viability of television versus radio versus print ads for different audiences. These issues, although relevant, are covered elsewhere. Instead, the focus of this book is on a topic I believe has received little attention in our industry—the practical development of a usable marketing plan. This isn't "cutting-edge" marketing, but rather very basic, grassroots marketing. Unfortunately, it is an area of marketing in which the healthcare industry could do a better job. In some ways, this is not a traditional book at all, but more of a cross between a guide and a workbook—but we'll talk more about that later.

The content of *Healthcare Marketing Plans That Work* can trace its roots back to my graduate school program at the Kellogg School at Northwestern University. During my two-year tenure, I studied many technical and theoretical areas of marketing. But it wasn't until I left school and secured a position in a provider organization that I came to realize I had never really learned how to write a viable marketing plan. In 1981, I was asked by my CEO to develop a "marketing plan" for a newly opened urgent care center. At that time, there was very little in the literature on the area of healthcare marketing. As a source of inspiration (desperation?) I went back to my graduate school textbooks—and discovered they really weren't very much help. They showed examples that focused on retail pricing, distribution of products from the manufacturer through warehouses to retail outlets, or national ad campaigns involving millions of dollars—none of which were especially relevant to the urgent care center in question or the 300-bed hospital that owned it.

Over time, my experience with this type of effort increased and the model discussed in this book evolved. In 1991, I left the provider side and returned to the consulting field, concentrating mostly on strategic marketing engagements. In 1996, I developed the first version of a half-day workshop on healthcare marketing plans and in 1997 (and again in 1998) I presented this workshop at the annual meeting of the Society for Healthcare Strategy and Market Development. Following each of these programs (and a number of state and specialty society programs), I received requests for a marketing plan "guide," "template" or other format. This led to the concept of developing a workbook to assist healthcare marketers with the creation of viable marketing plans.

Despite the requests of some of my workshop participants (and my own desires), this is not a "template" for a marketing plan. Unfortunately, we can't create the marketing equivalent of tax preparation software—drop in your spreadsheet data and out pops a formatted marketing plan.

If I could find a way to do that, I would retire and buy the 32-foot boat I have my eye on. In the end, this workbook can provide you with examples and a format that should make the process much easier—but the key to success is your individual ability to see what the information means and how it translates to opportunities and actions. Marketing is still as much an art as it is a science.

The development of a marketing plan is appropriate for any level of healthcare provider, be it hospital, health plan, service line, freestanding urgent care center or medical group practice. Clearly, the complexities, data, issues, and opportunities vary by organization type, but the process is essentially the same. The keys to a successful marketing plan for any type of provider include the following:

- Support from all of the key players, including leadership, the marketing staff and the staff who actually have to implement the actions.
- An organizational recognition that the responsibility for marketing (and the marketing plan) rests with the entire organization and not just with the staff who possess the marketing title.
- A very solid understanding of the factors that drive the market—essentially what hinders or helps your target audiences use the services your organization can provide.
- The development of a position, as well as strategies, objectives and actions, that are logically connected to an understanding of the market. An action that has no connection to the issues facing the organization is a waste of time and resources.
- Using the plan (with successes and mistakes) and incorporating the marketing plan process into the ongoing culture of the organization. A one-time marketing plan, no matter how well done, is nowhere near as useful as a marketing plan that is revisited, updated and used year after year.

This workbook is organized around the following seven major sections or components of a marketing plan:

- *Marketing plan process.* What are the axioms, issues, advantages and disadvantages of doing a marketing plan?
- *Market audit.* What is going on in the marketplace that can impact the organization?
- *Market position.* Where, in the mind of the key audience, does (and can) the organization or service exist?
- *Market strategies.* What are the major avenues to follow to secure the market position?
- *Quantifiable market objectives.* How are we going to measure whether we have accomplished anything with our marketing efforts?
- *Market actions.* What are we going to do in the next 12 to 24 months?
- *Implementation and monitoring.* What are we going to do to actually implement the plan and to track/adjust it as time goes on?

This book uses an "FAQ" (frequently asked questions) format. I think this will serve as the quickest and easiest way to get at the important elements of each part of the marketing plan. A number of sections also contain examples to illustrate the types of information that can go into a marketing plan, or how a market objective or market action can be formatted. Once again, these are not templates. Ideally, the formats and examples will guide you in the creation of your own marketing plans, but you must apply your own information, interpretation and determination of appropriate directions, measurements and actions.

This book is not meant to be a text on the structure of marketing in the healthcare setting. A number of authors have tackled this issue in the past and have done a very good job of it. My objective is not to discuss the marketing motivations of per diem payment rates or the advantages of print advertising over television advertising or the viability of mail versus telephone patient satisfaction surveys. My purpose is to provide a viable approach for taking the knowledge that marketers in healthcare settings have and/or can obtain and structuring that knowledge into a "guide" for a year's worth of successful marketing implementation.

One final thought—there is no "right" or "wrong" way to develop a marketing plan and no perfect format for such a plan. If the culture of your organization calls for graphs rather than data tables, do it that way. If organizational policy demands a full executive summary, add one. If "objectives" have to be called "goals" or if "actions" are referred to as "tactics," it really doesn't matter. The important thing is to develop a plan that is acceptable and usable, because in the end experience makes for the best marketing plans and the best marketing implementation. The worst marketing plan is the one that was never created because no one was sure as to "how to do it." To borrow a phrase from a well-known sporting-goods company, "just do it." With luck, the examples in this book will make the process a bit easier for you.

Case Descriptions

A practical guide to the development of marketing plans is best illustrated with real information from real organizations. As a result, the examples and exercises used in this book come from organizations with which I have worked. Organizational identities have been disguised. The data used are also adjusted so that only the proportional relevance is the same. Please note that the names used below are meant to be generic. If I inadvertently used the name of your organization, I beg your indulgence.

That said, let me briefly introduce you to seven case organizations:

High Plains Health Maintenance Organization (HPHMO). High Plains Health Maintenance Organization is a for-profit plan covering approximately 25 counties in a Midwestern state. The HMO is primarily commercial, but it also offers a Senior HMO product that is gaining ground in the local market. At this time, the HMO has opted not to pursue the Medicaid market, even though the state is mandating managed care plan enrollment for its Medicaid clients by the end of the calendar year. HPHMO is part of a larger, vertically integrated delivery system that includes over 500 physicians, three hospitals, a number of free-standing testing and treatment sites, a home health agency and other provider entities. At this time, HPHMO has about 130,000 lives and is facing increasing competition from five or six regional and national health plans.

Uptown University Medical Center (UUMC). Uptown University Medical Center is a 750-bed tertiary/quaternary center with a national reputation for organ transplants, oncology and cutting-edge heart care. UUMC is located in a city of just over a million people with a main hospital campus (in a less-than-desirable portion of the city) and three "branded" suburban ambulatory care centers. The Medical Center sees 26,500+ inpatient admissions, 1,300+ open-heart surgery cases and 4,100 births per year, but surprisingly only 24,000+ emergency room (ER) visits per year. UUMC has a medical staff of 830, of whom 560 are salaried faculty physicians. There are also 180 residents in six residency programs. UUMC has teaching affiliations with a number of community hospitals in the area, but it is not part of any formal systems or networks. The Medical Center has no direct competition for its quaternary services, but it does face competition from two multihospital systems in its service area. There are more than 20 active managed care entities in the market and all of them have per case/per diem/DRG (diagnosis-related group) contracts with UUMC (though some limit usage of UUMC to tertiary and quaternary services due to cost). Physician capitation is growing in the market, but the UUMC faculty practice plan is behind area independent practice associations (IPAs) and physician hospital organizations (PHOs) in this activity.

St. Gerald Medical Center (SGMC). St. Gerald Medical Center is a 375-bed community teaching hospital located on the west side of a city of 500,000 people (in a metropolitan area of 1.5 million people). SGMC offers a full range of secondary and tertiary clinical services including open-heart surgery and radiation oncology. The Medical Center sees 15,500+ admissions, 350+ open-heart surgery cases and 1,600+ births per year. SGMC is also the trauma center for the west side of town and thus gets 60,000+ ER visits per year. SGMC has a medical staff of 520 and it owns the practices of 20 primary care physicians (PCPs). There are also 30 family practice and surgery residents, rotating from a nearby university-based program. SGMC owns a few nonacute entities (home care, one urgent care center, 50% of a diagnostic imaging center, among others) but over 90% of their revenue comes from the hospital. Competition comes from four equal size or smaller hospitals that cover portions of the SGMC service area. SGMC is part of a religious system, but it does not have any sister entities in its own metropolitan area. There are over a dozen active managed care entities in the market and SGMC has contracts with all but one plan. This plan, however, has over 60,000 lives and is exclusively tied to a hospital network that does not include SGMC. The Medical Center and its physicians have an organized PHO, but it is not very active.

Bayshore Hospital (BH). Bayshore Hospital is a 200-bed general community hospital located in a small city/suburban/rural area with a population of 120,000. BH offers a good range of primary and secondary clinical services, including a recently built cardiac catheterization lab. The hospital sees 8,500+ admissions, 1,200 births and 29,000+ ER visits per year. BH has a medical staff of 180 with some significant limitations or shortages in three or four subspecialty areas. The hospital owns 12 physician practices, all of which are primary care. BH has a number of off-campus facilities in the market for fitness, diagnostic testing, health education and similar services. The hospital also contract-manages the county health department clinic and the student health center of a major private university located a mile from BH. There is only one acute care competitor in the BH service area and it is a small-town facility one-quarter the size of BH. Other competition comes from larger facilities located in cities 45 to 60 minutes away from the BH community. There are eight managed care entities in the market, of which only three have any real volume. The BH PHO has contracts with all of the area entities and currently has 5,000 global capitation lives.

Wolfe Memorial Hospital (WMH). Wolfe Memorial is a 90-bed general community hospital located in a town of 12,000 people on the fringe of a metropolitan area of 250,000 people. The majority of the WMH service area is small town or rural, though many people in the area commute to the nearby city for work, shopping or recreation. WMH has a reputation for providing high-touch care and for doing a good job within its range of capabilities. The hospital sees 4,000+ admissions, 400 births and 21,000 ER visits per year. WMH has a medical staff of 55, of whom 30 are specialists with part-time offices in the local market. As a defensive move, the hospital recently purchased the practices of nine PCPs, including a four-physician group recently affiliated with a competitor. Except for these physician practices, WMH does not own any off-campus entities (though it does offer home care and occupational health). There are no acute care competitors in the WMH service area, but there are three large tertiary centers within 20 to 25 miles. There are 15+ active managed care plans in the area and WMH has discount or per diem contracts with all of them. There is some recent indication, however, that a number of the WMH-affiliated PCPs do not have provider contracts with some of the managed care organization (MCO) entities or are not taking any new MCO patients.

Central Valley Cardiology Associates (CVCA). Central Valley Cardiology Associates is the dominant provider of physician-based cardiology services in its market (a city/suburban area of 250,000 people about two hours from a top-10 city market). CVCA has 12 physicians in the group with two office locations. The group provides a wide range of in-office testing and runs (via contract) the cardiac cath lab at hospital A. The group primarily works at hospital A, with only one or two members maintaining courtesy privileges at hospitals B and C (which also has a cath lab). There are three other cardiology practices in the market, ranging from a solo to a group of four. The market has eight active MCO players, but CVCA has contracts (discount or fee schedule) with only three of them.

Polaris Occupational Health (POH). Polaris Occupational Health is the leading provider of occupational health and workers' compensation services in its market (a mid-size city and metro area of 800,000 people). Polaris is owned by a physician group of 10 physicians with a minority investment by one of the hospitals in the market. POH has five branded sites, which offer services that include employment screening, drug testing, physical therapy, work hardening, work-site safety evaluations and injury treatment. The organization also provides third-party administrator (TPA) services to manage the occupational health costs for over 100 area employers.

Summary of a Marketing Plan Format

The following is an outline of the format of a healthcare-based marketing plan:

- Executive Summary (Optional)

- Part One: Market Audit
    - ☐ Key Observations
    - ☐ Brief Analyses of Important Data Elements

- Part Two: Market Position

- Part Three: Market Strategies

- Part Four: Market Objectives

- Part Five: Market Actions
    - ☐ Summary Table
    - ☐ Summary of Funding and Manpower
    - ☐ Action Descriptions

- Part Six: Implementation and Monitoring

- Part Seven: Detailed Data Appendices (if needed)

The Marketing Plan Process

■ What Is Marketing?

This may seem like an irrelevant question, but is it really? Ask 100 managers for a definition of marketing and you are likely to get at least 50 definitions (and perhaps more). For the sake of setting a tone for this workbook relative to the scope of a marketing plan, consider the following definition. Marketing may be defined as the minimization of the hindrances that keep your key audiences from using your products, services and/or ideas, and the maximization of the "helps" that make it easier to use them. This definition does not mention advertising, pricing or any other specific traditional marketing tool. Essentially *anything* that impacts your ability to complete the desired transactions (coming to your medical office, buying your plan product, having the MRI done at your facility) is fair game for a marketing plan. To illustrate:

- An urban hospital regularly runs out of visitor/patient parking by 10 a.m., with the nearest parking over two blocks away (in an area where safety is a concern).

- During the height of open enrollment, an HMO's telemarketing operation takes up to 12 minutes to respond to calls coming in after 5 p.m.

- A hospital-owned freestanding surgery center is unable to quickly and routinely provide prices for plastic, ENT, orthopedic and other elective surgery procedures.

- A pediatric medical practice located in an affluent suburban area does not provide office hours after 4 p.m. or on weekends.

- An occupational health program conducts a direct mail campaign with a call-in response for a packet of information on dealing with new OSHA regulations—and then takes six weeks to get the packets out after the calls come in.

■ What Is a Marketing Plan?

A marketing plan is a document (and a process) that provides a blueprint for the marketing activities of an organization or entity. Like any good blueprint, it takes into account the environment facing the organization and delineates a series of strategies and actions to take advantage of that environment and/or to mitigate its negative aspects. Also like a good blueprint, the marketing plan does not attempt to nail down every specific detail, but rather leaves room for changes and creativity. To carry the metaphor a bit further, the blueprint of a house shows where the wall should go—but not what color to paint it or what pictures to put on it. A market action that calls for a direct mail effort aimed at employers (for occupational health services) defines who, when and even how much it will cost, but it does not presume to dictate the colors, design layout or content of the brochure.

For a marketing plan to be viable, it must be flexible but not fluid. A *flexible* marketing plan establishes a specific set of actions for the upcoming year, *which requires some foresight on the part of all areas of the organization that will need support*. Thus, the department that knows it is recruiting a new neurosurgeon six months from now (but fails to tell anyone) may have to settle for a profile in the existing publications and a press release for initial publicity. In turn, the plan must be flexible enough to allow for issues and opportunities that could not be foreseen when the plan was being developed. Thus, when a local employer with 5,000 employees unexpectedly contacts the hospital to request an on-site health fair (for which it is prepared to pay some of the costs), the plan must have room for the reallocation of resources. In contrast, a *fluid* plan is so loose as to allow almost any activity to fit within its parameters. This type of plan has little or no definition of time frames or specific activities beyond a single line mention (e.g., "support newly acquired primary care practices," with no definition of how, when, with what resources and by whom). In many ways, a plan that is too fluid allows the marketing to operate almost by osmosis—being almost totally reactive instead of at least moderately proactive.

Experience shows that the first marketing plan done by any organization is the hardest. What information is needed? How can that information be obtained? What is a market position? What actions should be taken? These are difficult questions to answer. Experience also shows, however, that the marketing plan effort has a learning curve—that the second, third and subsequent efforts get easier.

■ What Is the Difference Between a Strategic Plan and a Marketing Plan? Between a Marketing Plan and a Marketing Communications Plan?

A *strategic plan* defines the business direction of the organization. It focuses on the purpose of the organization, the types of services and products it will provide, how the organization will be governed, with whom the organization will partner and so forth. The strategic plan establishes the parameters for all other efforts and plans established by the entity.

A *marketing plan* is the blueprint for the marketing activities of the organization. It focuses on the strategies and actions needed to complete the transactions desired with designated target audiences. Within the framework of the definition of marketing noted above, the marketing plan may have a fairly broad range, but it must remain within the parameters set by the strategic plan.

A *marketing communications* plan defines the specifics of the communications efforts used by the organization, usually in the areas of advertising and public relations. It will define the target audiences, the desired results of the communications, the methodologies to be used, the specific messages, the media plan and other related elements. For many organizations (and marketers) the marketing communications plan is viewed as synonymous with the marketing plan. In reality, a marketing communications plan is a subset of the marketing plan, albeit a very large one and one that will likely consume a majority of the available marketing-related resources.

It is not unusual for the lines between a strategic plan and a marketing plan to blur. Their formats are often similar and they usually analyze much of the same information. The two plans can blur even more if the organization lacks a well-defined strategic plan. In these cases, the marketing plan tends to move in the direction of "filling the vacuum." For a marketing plan to work, it needs to stay focused on the factors that minimize the "hindrances" and support the "helps." If factors outside of the traditional realm of marketing are impacting the ability of the organization to attract and/or retain business, they should be acknowledged in the marketing plan with the recognition that the solution may be politically beyond the scope of the plan. Here are some examples:

- All available information indicates a lack of convenient parking is hurting the image and usage of hospital A. This is noted as one of the strategies for change in the marketing plan, but the actual implementation rests with other parts of the organization.

- Input from members and employers indicates that a lack of OB/GYNs in County A is reducing interest in signing up with HMO X. This is noted in the marketing plan, but it is left to the provider relations function to implement provider recruitment activities.

What Is the Focus of a Marketing Plan?

The focus of a marketing plan is on the total organization, whether it be a group practice, service line, hospital, or health plan. *A good marketing plan is not just a marketing/public relations department work plan.* While much of the tactical marketing work will be done by the marketing function staff, the true measure of an organizationwide focus is the degree to which staff from across the entity are involved in the development and implementation of a marketing plan. Let's illustrate this with two examples from my consulting practice. One hospital ended up with a marketing plan that had 35 specific actions—of which 34 were the primary responsibility of marketing staff members. Another hospital had 40 specific actions, of which three were the responsibility of the CEO, one was the responsibility of the CFO (yes, the CFO), eight were the primary responsibility of various line and staff managers, and the balance (28) were the primary responsibility of the marketing staff. I can assure you that the marketing plan from the second hospital was more difficult to implement, but was much more successful in the long run.

■ How Much Detail Is Needed in a Marketing Plan?

There are different schools of thought on this and there is probably no "right" answer. Some organizations attempt to define every possible detail in their marketing plans. In my opinion this is a mistake, for two reasons. First, trying to dot every "i" and cross every "t" slows down the process—and the ultimate objective of the effort is to implement, not to create planning documents. Second, going into too much detail during the planning process reduces the ability of the implementing staff to use their abilities and creativity.

The market audit usually requires only one or two pages per major information element examined. The ultimate aim here is to pull out a handful of information "nuggets" for use in the development of strategies and actions.

The market position and market strategies can usually be summarized in a few pages. A strategy statement is meant to be general and should require only a few sentences. The measurable objectives can usually be handled in a couple of pages.

This leaves the market action, which is where many organizations tend to go into too much detail. Again, one or two pages is sufficient to describe the scope, timing, resource requirements and responsible parties for any marketing action. The more involved details should be handled when the action is actually implemented.

■ What Is a Reasonable Time Frame for a Marketing Plan?

In the late 1970s, most states in this country had entities called health systems agencies. By law, these agencies required hospitals to complete and file five-year strategic plans. Even in those days most of us in the field recognized the fiction involved in projecting plans out over a five-year period. Today, most of the strategic plans seen in the healthcare field look out over a two- to three-year period. Since a marketing plan should follow the parameters established by the strategic plan, its time frame cannot go out longer than the strategic plan's time frame.

With that in mind, a time frame of 12 months (a fiscal or calendar year, for example) is appropriate for a marketing plan. Some organizations push the plan frame to 18 to 24 months, but in reality, any activities scheduled beyond the 18-month horizon are questionable in terms of their likelihood of implementation. The marketing plan should be developed for a single year period and then reviewed and updated for each subsequent year.

■ What Are the Benefits of Having a Marketing Plan?

Given the number of organizations in this industry that regularly develop and use marketing plans, there are some solid benefits to the exercise. Here are some to consider:

- The marketing plan provides guidance for all marketing activities performed by the organization. If done well, it helps to minimize (but probably can't eliminate) the reactive marketing mode seen in many healthcare organizations.

- A marketing plan is the glue that connects the collective marketing intelligence and wisdom of the organization to the specific strategies, objectives and actions. This is called the rationale: in other words, are we doing something that makes sense in light of the market situation?

- The marketing plan is the focal point for all marketing systems—communications vehicles, community events, telemarketing, Web pages, customer satisfaction tracking, databases, and market research, among others.

- The marketing plan is the mechanism for formally determining time frames and schedules, assigning responsibilities and determining the resources needed to support the marketing effort for the upcoming year. When the plan is done, the marketing budget is also essentially done.

- Finally, a marketing plan (if done well) can serve as the catalyst for enhancing the marketing-oriented culture of the organization.

■ What Are the Limitations of Having a Marketing Plan?

While the benefits of doing and using a marketing plan are solid, there are also some limitations and downsides. These include the following:

- Developing a viable marketing plan takes experience and practice. This process is rarely taught in any detail in formal marketing education programs.

- Developing a marketing plan takes time and resources (staff time, market research and potentially even external support). For an organization that is stretched to the limit just to keep up with the market, the concept of taking time and effort to "do a plan" may not sit well. The creation of a marketing plan (especially the first time around) may not be rocket science, but neither is it a one-hour activity on an airplane trip to a conference.

- Marketers tend to be creative, energetic individuals, which is often what makes them valuable to their respective organizations. This type of personality is often one that likes to freewheel and shoot from the hip. The creation of a formal marketing plan can be restricting to this type of individual or organizational style.

- Finally, the hallmark of a good plan is to assign responsibilities for specific actions to clearly designated individuals. If there is a desire not to be personally responsible, the existence of a marketing plan can be uncomfortable.

■ How Do You Get Organized to Develop a Marketing Plan?

It almost sounds like an oxymoron ("getting organized to develop a plan"), but there are some issues up front that should be addressed before the marketing plan process begins. These include the following:

- *Involve the organization's leadership.* The leadership of the organization must, at a minimum, be supportive of the concept of developing a marketing plan. Ideally, the leadership should be involved in reviewing and approving key observations (see the market audit section), the market position, the strategies and even the objectives. Beyond a general review, however, the leadership should not be significantly involved in all of the details of the market actions. Managers, by their nature, want to put their stamp on tactical activities, even if it is not their area of expertise. Clearly, this situation will vary by organization. The physician partners in a 15-physician group are much more likely to be involved in this level of detail than the CEO of a 500-bed hospital. In general, however, the plan process will work out better if this approach is followed.

- *Have the needed background data in hand.* This is especially true for the first marketing plan effort. The market audit portion of the planning process requires a significant amount of background data. Rarely are these data conveniently at hand, in the desired format. Locating (or getting permission to use) the required information can often take weeks. Thus, this work should be done up front as much as possible, to avoid delays later on.

- *Anticipate the need for original research.* If primary research is needed to support the marketing plan, this effort should be initiated as soon as possible before the formal planning period. A key audience telephone survey (consumer, members, referring physicians, etc.) can take four to seven weeks to complete, while focus groups can take up to three to four weeks to complete.

- *Time the marketing plan right.* Because the marketing plan should serve as the basis for the development of the marketing budget for the year, it makes reasonable sense to complete or update the marketing plan *before* the submission of the annual budget. On the surface, this would seem self-evident, but it is not unusual to find healthcare organizations doing marketing plans well after the budgets have been approved for the year—not unlike closing the barn door after the horses have escaped.

- *Allow sufficient time.* The first time an organization develops a formal marketing plan, the process usually takes 60 to 90 days. This can be impacted by many factors, including data availability, research efforts, and the availability of key individuals for input and review, among others. Subsequent updates should go much more quickly, but 30 days is still a safe estimate.

- *Decide on the use of internal versus external resources.* This is an ongoing debate for almost every organization: should we (or can we) do the marketing plan with internal resources or is some degree of external help needed? The primary advantage of using internal resources is the cost savings. The counterpoints, however, include issues such as internal expertise (especially if this is the first time), internal staff time and internal objectivity. Many organizations opt to use some degree of external help the first time around and then internalize the process (with a limited degree of external oversight) for future updates. In the end, however, the course taken will depend on the needs and culture of each individual healthcare organization.

■ Why Do Marketing Plans Fail ... Or Succeed?

There are any number of reasons why a marketing plan will succeed or fail. Some are very obvious and tangible. Others are far more subjective. Here are 12 reasons that seem to come up over and over again—and occur in all types of healthcare (and nonhealthcare) organizations:

- *The marketing plan is not tied to other, equally important plans, such as the organization's strategic plan or master facility plan.* For example, if the strategic plan places a strong emphasis on supporting the development of a strong primary care physician base in outlying markets, the market plan must recognize this direction and provide appropriate support, such as research and target advertising. As another example, say a hospital's master facility plan calls for the renovation of the OB area beginning in 6 months, to last for a period of 12 months. During this time period, only 80% of the area's capacity will be available at any given time. The marketing plan needs to recognize the need for construction communication support and reopening support, as well as the likelihood that volumes may drop during the height of the renovation work.

- *The organization's leadership does not recognize the need or is just not interested in a formal marketing plan.* This is an unfortunate fact of life in too many organizations. The leadership does not perceive the need for any formalization of the marketing effort or sees marketing as a reactive tool—one that is used when "needed" and then usually only for communications-related support. Sometimes this problem can be overcome by a combination of education and small victories (a plan for a specific area or program that is successfully implemented). In many cases, however, a change in culture will not come until there is a change in leadership.

- ***The persons responsible for the implementation of the plan are not involved in the development of the plan.*** All actions must be assigned to someone (or a group of staff members) who are then responsible for the actual implementation. Ideally, many of the responsible individuals are *not* in the formal marketing function or department. To not involve these individuals in the development of the market actions (their scope, timing, resource requirements and tracking) at best invites indifference and at worst brings on outright opposition.

  For example, a few years ago when a national provider of specialty outpatient services developed a marketing plan, four specific actions were assigned to a newly hired national medical director. Unfortunately, no one saw fit to sit down with this individual to obtain his input or even his recognition of the responsibility. A year passed and the planning group got together to review results and begin the design of the marketing plan for the next year. The medical director, reviewing the old plan, noted that Actions C-1 to C-4 looked like good ideas—and wondered out loud why they had not been implemented. After an embarrassed moment, the entity's marketing vice president noted that he (the medical director) had been assigned that responsibility. Fortunately, the medical director had a good sense of humor; nonetheless, an entire year of opportunity had been lost due to the failure to involve the responsible implementers.

- ***The marketing plan is based on poor data or poor interpretation of the data.*** This is another variation on the old theme of "garbage in, garbage out." Clearly, marketing strategy or action decisions based on faulty information are likely to yield less than optimal results. In one case, the sampling plan for a hospital-conducted community attitude was not well designed—seniors were overrrepresented, resulting in a biased analysis. The hospital believed that its awareness, preference and image were much stronger than they actually were (especially among younger consumers).

- ***Staff turnover causes a lack of continuity.*** In recent years, the rate of turnover among senior healthcare managers has become quite high. This includes the senior marketing executives in all types of healthcare organizations. It is not unusual for the new leadership and/or marketing staff to have very little ownership of the marketing plan created by their predecessors.

- ***The objectives established for the marketing plan are unrealistic.*** Market objectives are the quantifiable, measurable targets that are being aimed for by the organization, such as enrollees, ER market share, number of referral sources or preference share. A marketing plan can fail if the objectives established are wholly unrealistic given the resources available, level of competition and time allowed.

  For example, a freestanding surgery center determined that it had 10% of the outpatient surgery volume in a finite market and established a target objective of getting to

20% in two years. In light of the facility capacity of the surgery center and the number of competitors, this was an unrealistic expectation. Over the two-year period, the center grew from 10% share to nearly 13% share. By industry standards, this was a very strong gain, but it appeared to be a failure based on the unrealistic objective established in the original marketing plan.

- ***The market actions are not technically, physically or legally achievable.*** I have not seen this too often in the healthcare sector, but it does occasionally happen that a planned action just cannot be implemented due to physical plant constraints, technical problems or outright legal restrictions. A good example here is an intended action by a Medicaid HMO to offer incentives to potential enrollees in the form of car seats, food vouchers and prepaid phone cards. This action was stopped by legal restrictions in that particular state, which limited enrollee incentives to $10 or less.

- ***The resources required to implement the actions are not available.*** For example, say the marketing plan calls for 8.0 FTEs and $1,500,000 in expenditures. The only problem is that the organization only has 3.0 FTEs and $500,000. Needless to say, the scope of the marketing plan will need to change.

- ***The market actions are not prioritized.*** As will be discussed in the market action section, if everything is a top priority then nothing is a top priority. The net result is the "deer in the car headlights" syndrome—everyone freezes and nothing happens.

  For example, a larger medical group developed a marketing plan with 20+ actions for the next year. All were deemed essential and none of the internal camps within the organization would compromise or give any ground. The end result was that virtually none of the actions were implemented.

- ***There are no time frames established for implementation of the market actions.*** It is essential to establish time frames for the implementation of the developed actions. Without this accountability, it's easy for staff members to ignore or delay the start of new actions in the face of the demanding day-to-day needs of most healthcare organizations.

  For example, a hospital failed to establish specific start times for the market actions in its plan. One month before the end of the target year, there was a hectic, disorganized attempt to catch up on the market actions, resulting in action failures, wasted resources and internal conflict and confusion.

- ***There are no established responsibilities for the implementation of specific market actions.*** A market action must be someone's clearly designated responsibility. Without this level of accountability, it is easy for the actions outlined in a marketing plan to fall between the cracks of day-to-day responsibilities.

For example, a large medical group established a plan with a dozen specific activities for the upcoming year, but no assignment of responsibility. By the end of the year, only one activity had been implemented—and that only because the administrative director of the group took a personal interest in the activity in question.

- *The marketing plan is never implemented and/or never becomes part of the organizational culture.* The healthcare field (and, for that matter, many others) is rife with examples of "shelf documents"—studies and reports that are created but never actually used. In my opinion, one of the key measures of success for a marketing plan is the degree to which the main copy (usually in the hands of the marketing director or vice president) looks dog-eared. Clearly, if the marketing plan is never implemented, it is a sign that the process was a failure. If the marketing process is not incorporated into the organizational culture, that is another indicator of a process failure. As a consultant, I see this all too often. External help is brought in to develop a marketing plan, but the process is not internalized and the plan is not updated and carried forward in future years.

■ What About Measuring Results and 'Return on Investment?'

I saved this one for last because it is probably the most hotly debated issue in the area of marketing and marketing plans in healthcare. I am a stickler for establishing quantifiable objectives for any marketing plan. I have come to the conclusion, however, that the absolute measurement of the return on investment (ROI) for any *single* marketing effort in healthcare is almost impossible.

This may sound like a contradiction in terms, but let me illustrate the point. St. Gerald Medical Center does a market audit and discovers that in its primary service area it has a 25% share of neurology and neurosurgery admissions and a 30% preference share among consumers for the care of neurological injuries and conditions. It sets an objective (over a two-year period) of growing market share to 30% and preference share to 40%. To do this, it implements the following actions: recruit three additional neurologists and two additional neurosurgeons (one with a national reputation); add/upgrade a number of testing devices; dedicate a specific space in the hospital as the "Neurosciences Center," with appropriate signage and collaterals; add a specific neurosciences module to its ongoing image advertising effort; add profiles of the neurosciences physicians to its community quarterly publication (which goes to 60,000 households); conduct a series of community and professional education seminars; get its neurosurgeon "star" onto a number of radio and television health talk shows, and so forth.

At the end of two years (or even at interim points), St. Gerald can look at its situation and objectively measure its progress in terms of market share and preference share. It may even be able to look at *all* the dollars put into the neurosciences effort and measure that against the additional revenues generated by the greater patient volumes to determine a global ROI. But there is probably no practical way to determine the ROI for each of the dozen or more distinct parts of the overall marketing plan for the neurosciences! Did the professional education courses contribute 17% of the gain in volume for a cost of $38,000? Did the physician profiles in the existing community publication contribute 8% of the gain for essentially no additional cost? We may want to know, but it probably isn't worth the time and effort to find out. Moreover, there may be no practical way to find out.

Why is the measurement of ROI for specific market actions so difficult in healthcare? Here are some of the reasons:

- Marketing effectiveness is the confluence of a variety of efforts and inputs and rarely the result of one specific ad or sales call or brochure. As marketers, we continually use our own experience and the experience of the industry to play with the marketing mix in an attempt to maximize the overall objective return.

- Unlike many other industries, most (but not all) healthcare decisions have a time lag. A soda jingle on the radio may influence my decision as I stop at the next convenience store for something to drink. In contrast, however, all of your efforts to build your cardiology services may influence my familiarity and preference, but it is unlikely to get me to use the service until I have a specific heart-related health need (which, with luck, will be years from now).

- By and large, healthcare organizations lack the resources and systems needed to track the specific returns for specific marketing efforts. If the organizational marketing budget is $800,000, it may be difficult to justify spending $100,000 of it on tracking systems.

There are, of course, exceptions to every rule. In some instances, it is possible (without an act of Congress) to measure the return from specific market actions in the same tactical category. For example, Polaris Occupational Health may find it difficult to measure the exact return on sales calls as compared with business leader seminars, trade shows and direct mail. It may be possible, however, for Polaris to measure the ROI from participation in trade shows A, B and C and determine that C consistently (over a four-year period) has produced far fewer contracts (and revenues) than the other two.

It may also be possible to measure the return from a specific, limited effort. For example, St. Gerald Medical Center works with a major department store to develop an in-store mammography suite. The effort (with promotion via direct mail, print ads and in-store signs) results in over 5,700 screenings in the first two years, with 50+ biopsies and 24 cancer cases. The financial return is just over $100,000 (after direct and indirect expenses) for the two-year period. In this case, the overall program could be measured for ROI—but how much was contributed from visibility versus signs versus direct mail, and so forth?

At this point, the reader should not assume that I am against attempting to measure the return on investment. What I am recommending is that healthcare organizations seeking to measure ROI should focus on:

- The achievement of more global marketing objectives
- The return on investment for the *total* mix of efforts put into a specific area
- The ROI for specific efforts within the same tactical category (in cases where determination of ROI does not cost more than the effort being measured)

At the time this book was finalized, there was a growing argument that one-to-one marketing efforts, including database mining (working with the records of individual consumers to discern potential future usage opportunities) might result in a greater ability to measure the exact return on a specific marketing effort. For a number of reasons, the jury is still out as to whether providers will be able to use database mining to the levels pioneered by American Express and other nonhealthcare firms. Until this type of marketing technique becomes routinely viable for healthcare entities, I will stick with the comments made above.

■ The Market Audit

■ What Is a Market Audit?

An audit is defined as a thorough examination and evaluation of a problem. A market audit is a detailed evaluation of all of the factors that influence the marketing situation facing an organization. For healthcare marketing plans, the market audit looks at two major, related areas: the status of the market environment facing the organization and the functionality of the marketing systems within the organization.

■ What Should You Include?

Everything and anything. Remember the definition of marketing that was used above. Any factor that helps or hinders the ability of key audiences to use your services is worth looking at. It is better to look at an issue or data element and determine that it tells you nothing of value than to skip over it and learn later that you missed a key issue that would impact the marketing strategies for the next year.

Appendix A provides a list of data elements that should be examined in a typical hospital marketing plan effort. In addition, here are some general categories of information worth considering for a market audit. This is not intended to be an all-inclusive list, but it's a good starting point.

Environmental Data

- Strategic plan goals
- Service area definition
- Key audience structure
- Service area demographics
- Employer mix (size, industry, insurers)
- Facility locations, hours, access, condition
- Medical staff/provider panel structure
- Referral sources, volumes
- Historical activity levels
- Payer mix
- MCO pricing arrangements
- Market share
- Competitor profiles
- Sales systems and activity
- Communications activities, budgets, outlets
- Community education classes and events
- Key audience research

Marketing Systems

- Key audience satisfaction tracking
- Ease of access to/completeness of marketing databases
- Consistency of graphics, name usage
- Completeness and current nature of collaterals and sales support materials
- Publication distribution and readership
- Centralized sales databases
- Sales effectiveness—calls made, leads generated, contracts closed
- Marketing budgets as a percentage of overall revenues and compared with competitors
- Inquiry/order fulfillment systems (timeliness, accuracy)
- Press relations/media coverage
- Event participation
- Advertising effectiveness—recall, awareness, response, etc.
- Enrollment/reenrollment systems and rates
- Medical call centers—access, response time, types of calls
- Web page—ease of use, timely information, passive and active usage
- Completeness of marketing plan implementation

■ What Is the Format?

Limit the analysis of any one data element (such as demographics, sales force activities, or payer mix) to one or two pages, if possible. Some elements (such as a summary of a consumer survey) may require a bit more space, but remember that the intention is to do a summary, not a direct transcription of the raw data tables. A reasonable market audit for a hospital, medical group, or HMO can usually be completed in 40 to 50 pages covering 15 to 20 categories of information.

Provide a brief description of the data element in question. Summarize the data in a few bullet points or in a brief table or chart. If a table/chart is used, provide a few bullets highlighting the key points from the table. If the data element in question comes from a massive report or 100-page printout, reference that report for the few individuals who really want to learn more. Add the extra detail as an appendix or supplementary report if absolutely necessary.

There is no right way to conduct this type of analysis and presentation. The important point is not to bury the user in data but rather to get to the point—enough summary information to highlight the issue, and the key observations as to what the data really mean.

■ Snapshots versus Trends

The market audit should focus on trends over time as opposed to snapshots of a particular issue. Trend patterns have much more meaning for marketing purposes than a single element in a single three-month quarter; for example:

- The trend of responses for all promotional efforts for the year is more meaningful than the return on a single direct mail effort.

- Trends in the ER payer mix for the past three years are more useful than the payer mix for ER services in the fourth quarter.

- Referrals by physician for the past three years should be addressed rather than referrals to the open-heart surgery program by physician for the past year.

Avoid overreacting to changes in patterns for a short, finite period, both for the development of a marketing plan and for normal marketing tracking purposes. For example, referral tracking to a specialty medical group may show that PCP Group 6 normally refers 50 patients per year to the group. The first quarter of this year shows only three referrals, but by the second quarter the volume is back up to 15—on track again for 50+ for the year. Informal contact shows that PCP Group 6 moved its office in the first quarter and thus their volume was down.

■ What Is a 'Key Observation?'

There is a quote from Mark Twain that neatly describes the relationship between data and "key observations." It goes:

> *"Thunder is good. Thunder is impressive. But it is the lightning that does the work."*

Data are good. A lot of data, laid out in a nice format, can be very impressive (and very confusing). But, in the end, we need to know what in the world it means. This is where we come to the "key observations."

A key observation is a short (three- to five-sentence) summary of what a particular finding means or why it is important to the organization. If there is an area of "art" in the development of a marketing plan, it lies in the ability to pull key observations from reams of raw data. It is essential that the effort be made to pull the important observations from the audit data, however, since these form the basis from which the market position, strategies and actions are developed.

All of the key observations may be pulled out and grouped together under a specific heading at the front of the market audit section. In this format they essentially serve as an "executive summary" for the market audit.

There is no magic number of key observations for any plan. Each information section should have at least one, but some (such as a key audience survey) could have many. In preparation for this book, I reviewed a number of recently completed marketing plans for healthcare provider entities. The average was 45 to 50 key observations per plan.

One final point on key observations—they need to be "key." In other words, they need to illustrate a point that is important to the marketing direction of the organization and quickly provide the reader with a useful insight about the market situation.

The best way to illustrate this is by the following key observation: *"The team that has scored the first goal has won seven out of the fourteen World Cup finals."* Sounds pretty impressive until you realize that it says nothing useful. All it says is that if you score the first goal in the World Cup final, you have a 50/50 chance of winning or losing. Not a very helpful observation if you are the coach planning out game strategies! By the way, this statement was actually made during the international television broadcast of the men's World Cup Soccer final in 1998.

■ Do You Have Some Examples?

Well, sure we do—it wouldn't be much fun without them. The balance of this chapter has a number of market audit sections adapted from actual plans. Each one is an abbreviated but self-contained summary of important data from that organization or its local market. Please note that the "introduction" to each example is for the convenience of the reader and would likely not be phrased in the same manner for an actual market audit section.

After each information section, there is a "key observation" resulting from the data. While these key observations are on the same page as the data, they are most effective when grouped together into a summary section at the front of the market audit portion of the plan.

Market Audit Example One—St. Gerald Medical Center Service Area Definition (IP)

The following table is a summary of the number of cases and percent of overall inpatient cases that came to St. Gerald from the primary and secondary service areas (and all other areas) over the most recent three-year period.

Area	1997 Cases	1997 Percent	1998 Cases	1998 Percent	1999 Cases	1999 Percent
33324	3,199	20.4%	3,211	20.6%	3,202	20.5%
33325	1,788	11.4%	1,729	11.1%	1,745	11.2%
33327	1,235	7.9%	1,241	8.0%	1,249	8.0%
33339	977	6.2%	921	5.9%	950	6.1%
33341	819	5.2%	832	5.4%	924	5.9%
33321	645	4.1%	735	4.7%	751	4.8%
All other PSA	2,809	17.9%	2,840	18.3%	2,871	18.5%
Primary Area	**11,472**	**73.1%**	**11,509**	**74.0%**	**11,692**	**75.0%**
33319	150	0.9%	148	0.9%	143	0.9%
33359	145	0.9%	150	1.0%	148	0.9%
33311	143	0.9%	139	0.9%	141	0.9%
33367	139	0.9%	127	0.8%	125	0.8%
33312	137	0.9%	121	0.8%	121	0.8%
33365	131	0.8%	129	0.8%	119	0.8%
All other SSA	2,010	12.9%	1,922	12.4%	1,853	11.9%
Secondary Area	**2,855**	**18.2%**	**2,736**	**17.6%**	**2,650**	**17.0%**
Out of Area	1,365	8.7%	1,302	8.4%	1,247	8.0%
Total	15,692	100.0%	15,547	100.0%	15,589	100.0%

Note: All zip codes noted are for example purposes only.

Key Observation

- **The percentage of inpatient cases coming from the primary service area (PSA) is steadily increasing, while the percentage of cases coming from the secondary service area (SSA) and beyond is steadily decreasing. This suggests that St. Gerald is losing ground as a regional medical facility and is relying more and more on its PSA for patient volume.**

■ Market Audit Example Two—Results Tracking/Polaris OccHealth Advertising

Polaris Occupational Health routinely advertises its services to employers in the metropolitan area served. The following table summarizes the results of the advertising used for the most recent 12-month period.

Media Used	Cost (1)	Qualified Leads (2)	Cost Per Lead	Contracts (3)	Cost Per Contract
Direct Mail	$50,000	115	$ 435	14	$ 3,571
Print—Newspaper	$40,000	50	$ 800	9	$ 4,444
Print—Business Journal	$25,000	30	$ 833	19	$ 1,315
Radio	$60,000	15	$4,000	1	$60,000

(1) Production and media placement.
(2) Qualified lead is defined as a contact from an individual who has the authority to determine the occupational health services contract for a specific organization.
(3) Defined as a specific contract for healthcare services in excess of $1,000 per year.

Key Observation

- **Radio advertising may not be an effective part of the advertising media mix for Polaris. Consideration should be given to shifting funds to other media.**

■ Market Audit Example Three—Marketing Grid Summary/Bayshore Hospital

The following is a partial summary of the results of the marketing grid (see appendix C) done for Bayshore Hospital:

<u>Publications</u>. The following publications are produced by the Bayshore Public Relations Office:

- *Around The Halls.* A bimonthly publication distributed at 30+ points within the organization to hospital employees, volunteers, physicians and other internal parties. Circulation is 1,000 per issue. Focus is on operational news, promotions, new employees and related topics.

- *The Bayshore Magazine.* Published two or three times per year, as resources allow. Distributed by mail to a list of approximately 18,000 including patients from the most recent 12 months, employees, physicians, volunteers, donors and civic leaders. Focus is on new services, facility renovations, new physicians to the staff and similar topics.

- *Bayshore Volunteers.* Published quarterly and distributed by mail to approximately 600 volunteers. Public Relations handles layout and production. Volunteer coordinator develops all copy and maintains list.

Key Observation

- **All of Bayshore's publications are internally focused or focused on the immediate "family." The organization lacks any regular outlets to key audiences such as area consumers, medical staff members and employers. In addition, the employee-oriented publications are spaced too far apart to be used effectively for timely information dissemination.**

■ Market Audit Example Four—Capture Rate/High Plains HMO

High Plains, as with most managed care products, faces two stages in its sales effort. The first is to sell the plan to the employer. The second (in 50% to 75% of the cases) is to sell the plan to the employees in the face of competition from other plans offered by the employer. The following table summarizes the historical volumes for High Plains for the past four years.

Year	Employers Contracted	Eligible Employees	High Plains Enrollees (1)	Capture Rate
1996	819	76,125	35,398	46.5%
1997	865	83,295	37,982	45.6%
1998	934	89,655	39,717	44.3%
1999	1,002	94,260	40,720	43.2%

Key Observation

- **On the surface, High Plains is gaining ground every year—more contracts, more eligible employees, more enrollees. At the same time, however, the capture rate (the percentage of eligible employees who actually enroll) is steadily declining. Whatever the reasons, this is a marketing threat for the organization. (Note: If the 1996 capture rate held in 1999, High Plains would have 3,100 additional enrollees. At a value of over $2,000 per enrollee due to dependent coverage, this translates into over $6.2 million in lost premiums per year.)**

Market Audit Example Five—Bayshore Hospital Medical Staff Distribution

Part of the market audit analysis of the Bayshore Medical Staff includes a review of the geographic distribution of the offices of these physicians. The following table summarizes this distribution. Bayshore is located in zip code 75601 and has an eight-zip-code PSA and a six-zip-code SSA divided into a north and south cluster of three zip codes each.

Zip Code/Area	Primary Offices	Percent of Primary Offices	Specialty Offices	Percent of Specialty Offices
75601	48	72%	93	74%
75602	12	18%	16	13%
Balance of PSA	4	6%	9	7%
Secondary North Service Area	2	3%	1	1%
Secondary South Service Area	1	1%	0	0%
Other Areas	0	0%	6	5%

Note: All zip codes noted are for example purposes only.

Note: Each physician is allocated one or more office locations. Thus, three PCPs in the same office are counted as three primary offices.

Key Observation

- **Nearly 90% of the offices of the medical staff members of Bayshore Hospital are within one or two miles of the hospital campus. There is virtually no access to physicians actively associated with Bayshore in the SSA. Consumers who want to use Bayshore must essentially drive to the hospital campus area to see an affiliated physician. From parts of the PSA and the entire SSA this involves 15 to 30 minutes of travel. This leaves Bayshore vulnerable to interception by physicians placed by competing facilities.**

Market Audit Example Six—Referral Patterns for Central Valley Cardiology Associates

The following table summarizes the referrals by physician and group to the Central Valley Cardiology Associates for a two-year period. The table also shows the managed care plan panels in which the various referral sources participate. Central Valley has provider contracts with only MCOs 1, 5 and 7.

MD Group	1998 Referrals	1999 Referrals	MCO Plans	Notes
Smith & Jones FPs	24	11	1,2,3,4,6,8	
Northside IMs	38	22	1,3,4,5,6,7,8	Bought by Hospital C
Dr. Williams (IM)	6	1	2,3,4,6,8	
Oak Hill FPs	61	64	1,2,3,4,5,7,8	Owned by Hospital A
Centerville IMs	38	23	2,4,5,6,8	One physician retired
Westside FPs	45	61	1,2,3,4,6,7,8	Opened site in Central Valley's building
FPs of Columbia	32	21	2,3,4,5,6,7,8	Bought by Hospital C
Downtown IMs	21	7	2,3,4,6,8	
Rose, West FPs	16	8	1,3,4,5,6,8	Bought by Hospital C
River Associates (FP and IM)	112	81	1,2,3,4,6,8	
Elm Street FPs	41	32	2,3,4,5,7,8	
Valentine, Post and Johnson, PC	24	36	1,2,3,4,5,6,8	Recently purchased by Hospital A
Hillside Clinic (FP and IM)	78	61	2,3,4,6,7,8	Bought by Hospital C
Jensen & Levine FPs	2	21	1,2,3,4,6,7,8	Newly formed group in CVCA's building
Water Street Clinic	62	41	2,3,4,5,6,8	Recently added part-time cardiologist to group
All Other Sources	281	311		
All Sources	**881**	**801**		

Key Observations

- **Hospital C is purchasing primary care groups that historically refer to Central Valley. Central Valley physicians are not active at Hospital C and it is very likely that the hospital is requesting the newly acquired groups to shift their referral patterns to cardiologists associated with Hospital C.**

- **Managed care plans 1, 5 and 7 have much lower participation rates among the PCPs who actively refer to Central Valley. The PCP physicians are likely facing restrictions on referral patterns to specialists who are not participants in the MCO panels**

Market Audit Example Seven—Patient Satisfaction Patterns by Nursing Unit at Uptown University

Uptown University Medical Center conducts a monthly survey of patient satisfaction for all units of the hospital. University uses a service line format, and thus patients in major clinical areas are almost always on specific nursing units. The following is the pattern of patient satisfaction scores by unit for the past six quarters (the scale used is 1 to 5, with 5 equivalent to "excellent").

Unit/Area	Q1/98	Q2/98	Q3/98	Q4/98	Q1/99	Q2/99
Emergency	3.81	3.90	3.77	3.84	3.81	3.91
Outpatient Surgery	4.50	4.55	4.58	4.55	4.49	4.54
Urgent Care Center	4.11	4.16	4.59	4.49	4.60	4.63
2N – Obstetrics	4.41	4.38	4.35	4.40	4.33	4.41
2S – Pediatrics	4.79	4.81	4.78	4.85	4.83	4.86
3N – Cardiology	4.25	4.30	4.32	4.32	4.29	4.33
3S – General Med/Surg	4.39	4.41	4.40	4.35	4.39	4.34
4N – Orthopedics	4.10	4.15	4.16	4.11	4.08	4.14
4S – General Med/Surg	4.29	4.35	4.36	4.27	4.31	4.35
5N – Oncology	4.45	4.41	4.04	3.82	3.40	3.39
5S – General Med/Surg	4.28	4.35	4.32	4.27	4.38	4.31
6N – Gynecology	3.05	3.11	3.08	3.01	3.10	3.02
6S – General Med/Surg	3.12	3.09	3.13	3.15	3.11	3.15

Key Observations

- **Patient satisfaction with the on-campus urgent care center improved noticeably after the opening of the dedicated parking lot (May 1998).**

- **Patient satisfaction with the pediatric unit is consistently the highest in the organization. This may serve as a value-added selling point for the pediatric service line at Uptown.**

- **Patient satisfaction with the oncology unit dropped noticeably in the third quarter of 1998. The clinical leadership and staffing patterns for this unit changed in the second quarter of 1998.**

- **Patient satisfaction scores for both units on the 6th floor are significantly below all other measured inpatient units. The 6th floor has not been renovated per the 1996 master facility plan and facility upgrade efforts. This upgrade is scheduled for the 2nd quarter of 2000.**

Market Audit Example Eight—Preference Share versus Market Share/ St. Gerald PSA

In a recent consumer survey, St. Gerald measured preference share (where consumers preferred to go) and reported market share (where they actually went) for a number of clinical service areas. The following table highlights the results for the St. Gerald PSA.

Service	Preference Share	Market Share	Differential
Inpatient Adult Med/Surg	59%	61%	-2%
Inpatient or Outpatient Oncology Care	71%	60%	+11%
Inpatient or Outpatient Cardiology Care	74%	63%	+11%
Inpatient or Outpatient Pediatric Care	41%	63%	-22%
Obstetrical Care	68%	67%	+1%
Emergency Services	50%	77%	-27%
Outpatient Surgery	49%	71%	-22%

Key Observations

- **There is some degree of consumer desire to use St. Gerald for oncology and cardiology services over and above actual market share. There is an opportunity to capture additional volumes in these two areas if the hindrances to usage can be determined and removed.**

- **St. Gerald has a strongly negative position in terms of public preference versus actual usage for pediatric care, emergency services and outpatient surgery. A significant number of PSA consumers would use another option if it became available to them (or they will actively seek out other options when they need this type of care).**

■ Market Audit Example Nine—Advertising Recall/St. Gerald

In the same consumer survey, St. Gerald tested consumer advertising recall of healthcare advertising. The table below highlights the recall rate of advertising sponsorship by healthcare providers in the market.

Ad Sponsor	1995 Survey	1997 Survey	1999 Survey
St. Gerald	31%	29%	17%
Memorial	18%	20%	30%
Community Regional	17%	17%	25%
Northside	10%	10%	8%
Other	15%	14%	12%
Unsure	9%	10%	8%

Key Observation

- **St. Gerald has lost its leadership position in terms of healthcare advertising recall in the marketplace. This may reflect a combination of problems in advertising budgets, media effectiveness and advertising message effectiveness.**

Market Audit Example Ten—MCO Panel Participation by Wolfe Memorial Physicians

Wolfe Memorial has provider contracts with all known HMO and PPO entities in its market (a total of 14 plans). Using plan provider directories and interviews with physician office staffs, the hospital prepared the following analysis of plan provider panel membership by Wolfe-affiliated PCPs.

MD/Plan ▶	1	2	3	4	5	6	7	8	9	10	11	12	13	14	15
FP 1		*					*				*				*
FP 2	*						*		*		*			*	*
FP 3		x					x		x					x	x
FP 4		*													
FP 5		*					*				*		*		*
FP 6	*	*		*					*				*	*	*
FP 7		*					*		*					*	*
OB/GYN 1	x	x		x			x		x	x			x	x	x
OB/GYN 2		*					*	*			*		*	*	*
OB/GYN 3		*						*					*		
Peds 1	*	*		*		*	*	*			*		*	*	*
Peds 2	*	*		*		*	*	*			*		*	*	*
Peds 3	x	x						x			x		x	x	x
Peds 4									*				*		
IM 1	x	x					x		x					x	x
IM 2		*					*				*			*	*
IM 3		*		*			*		*		*		*		*

Legend

Blank space   No contract/not on panel.

*   On panel/taking new patients

x   On panel/not taking new patients

Key Observation

- **Although Wolfe Memorial has active contracts with all of the MCO entities in the market, the primary care physician base at the hospital is not well positioned relative to provider contracts. A number of plans have no Wolfe Memorial-affiliated PCPs on their panels and many have very limited PCP availability. This lack of PCP participation could seriously impact Wolfe by reducing consumer access to the hospital's services as managed care enrollment volume grows.**

Market Audit Example Eleven—Outpatient Surgery Patient Satisfaction at Wolfe Memorial

The internal patient satisfaction measurement system used by Wolfe Memorial shows that the ratings for outpatient surgery are in line with or better than the ratings for most of the other functions of the hospital. In addition, the ratings for Wolfe's outpatient surgery services are consistent over a two-year period (with quarterly measurements). During a recent community survey, Wolfe asked consumers who had used outpatient surgery services at Wolfe and a number of other area facilities to rate their satisfaction with that experience. The following table summarizes the findings.

Facility	Number of Users	Rating (1)
All Users/All Facilities	335	3.09
Wolfe Memorial	135	2.65
Community Regional (2)	45	3.21
St. John's (2)	39	3.19
North General (2) (4)	21	3.41
Riverside SurgiCenter (3)	85	3.29

(1) Rating was done on a 1 to 4 scale, with 1 = very dissatisfied, 2 = somewhat dissatisfied, 3 = somewhat satisfied, and 4 = very satisfied.
(2) Urban tertiary centers about 20 miles away from Wolfe's market.
(3) Suburban facility located between Wolfe's community and the urban market.
(4) Results should be used with caution due to sample size.

Key Observation

- **While the patient satisfaction ratings for Wolfe Memorial's outpatient surgery function have been consistent over time, the scores come in significantly lower than the ratings for all the competitors. This is likely contributing to the noticeable out-migration for outpatient surgery services. (Note: Follow-up open-ended questions indicate that the primary reasons for patient dissatisfaction with Wolfe are long waiting times, a lack of certain surgical capabilities and perception of small, uncomfortable facilities.)**

Market Audit Example Twelve—Preference Share Patterns for Uptown University

As part of a consumer research effort, Uptown University Medical Center measured consumer preference (inpatient services) for Uptown and its major competitors in both the primary service area (a two-county area including and surrounding a major city) and the secondary service area (12 counties divided into four subareas). The following results were found:

Hospital	PSA	SSA – A (1)	SSA – B (2)	SSA – C (3)	SSA – D (4)
St. Mary's	31%	9%	11%	9%	12%
Johnson	21%	7%	6%	7%	5%
Community Memorial	18%	4%	4%	2%	1%
Uptown	10%	29%	21%	23%	20%
Other Hospitals (5)	16%	2%	1%	1%	2%
Local Hospitals (6)	N/A	41%	48%	51%	50%
Other/Unsure	4%	8%	9%	7%	10%

(1) SSA Counties 1, 2 and 3 (north of PSA)
(2) SSA Counties 4, 5 and 6 (north and east of PSA)
(3) SSA Counties 7, 8 and 9 (east and south of PSA)
(4) SSA Counties 10, 11 and 12 (west of PSA)
(5) Other hospitals in the PSA (4 in all)
(6) Local hospitals based in the SSA counties (12 in total)

Key Observations

- **Uptown University Medical Center has a relatively weak preference share position in its PSA. (Note: When compared to actual market share, Uptown has a serious deficit.)**

- **Uptown University has a fairly strong preference share position in the SSA, well above that of any other facility based in the immediate urban market.**

- **Uptown has a very strong preference share position in the secondary area "A", especially in comparison to the local hospitals serving that market.**

■ Market Audit Example Thirteen—Access to a New Market/St. Gerald

The following is a summary of the analysis of a two-zip-code area including and around the town of New Market (about 20 miles from St. Gerald in the western fringe of the county).

Demographics

- Population—21,350 in 1999/24,550 projected for 2004
- Average household income—$52,375
- Percent commercial/managed care/Medicare insured—89%

Competition

- The New Market area is served by a 90-bed general community hospital. This hospital recently merged with one of St. Gerald's main competitors.

St. Gerald Situation

- St. Gerald draws 275 to 300 admissions per year from this area.
- St. Gerald averages a market share of 13% to 15% of inpatient volume from New Market. This places St. Gerald in second position behind the local facility.
- St. Gerald has only six physicians with active privileges in the New Market area. All are relatively low admitters. The majority of the patient volume to St. Gerald from this area comes via referrals to specialists affiliated with St. Gerald.
- Preference for St. Gerald among New Market area consumers is 10% to 15% higher than actual market share.

Access

- It currently takes 30 to 45 minutes to travel from New Market to St. Gerald via a U.S. Highway or an interstate connecting to local roads. A new extension of the Interstate will open in 10 to 12 months and is projected to cut travel time from New Market to the St. Gerald area to 15 to 20 minutes.

Key Observation

- **All of the individual factors (demographics, competition, entity situation and access) strongly suggest that New Market should be a priority target for St. Gerald.**

Market Audit Example Fourteen—Service Profit Margins and Pricing/Polaris OccHealth

The occupational health services market in the area served by Polaris is relatively price sensitive. As part of its market audit process, Polaris conducted an analysis of the profit margin of a number of its service offerings and the relative price position (percent above or below the market average) of those services. The following table highlights the results of this analysis.

Service	Profit Margin	Percent Above or Below Market
Pre-Employment – A	+11%	+2%
Pre-Employment – B	+12%	+3%
Pre-Employment – C	+10%	-2%
Drug Screening – A	+15%	+1%
Drug Screening – B	+13%	+2%
Specialty Exam – A	+6%	-20%
Specialty Exam – B	+18%	+3%
Specialty Exam – C	+12%	+5%
Specialty Exam – D	+15%	+6%
Worksite Toxicity	+9%	-1%
Executive Physicals – A	+20%	-3%
Executive Physicals – B	+26%	-5%
Work Hardening Series	+18%	+5%
Education Program – A	-20%	+10%
Education Program – B	-34%	+9%
Education Program – C	-21%	+11%

Key Observations

- **Polaris' pricing is well below the market average for specialty exam A. There may be room to raise prices and thus increase the profit margin for this service.**

- **Executive physicals provide very strong profit margins for Polaris. The exams provided by Polaris are slightly below the market average. There may be room to either raise fees slightly (for profit) or to lower fees even more (for market share).**

- **Educational offerings are losing money and are priced well above the market average. Consideration should be given as to whether these offerings should be retained in the Polaris mix of services.**

■ Market Audit Example Fifteen—Impact of Facility Renovations/Bayshore

The following is a summary of the Bayshore facility renovation project plan for the upcoming 36-month period.

Project	Start	Time Frame	Impact
Lobby Renovation	1/00	4 Months	Public access must be redirected, no waiting area, information desk in temporary location.
Parking Deck A Resurfacing	6/00	3 Months	Loss of 200 spaces (visitor and patient) at most times.
Nursing Unit Cosmetic Upgrades (4 Units)	3/00	16 Months (4 months per unit)	One full Med/Surg nursing unit (30 beds) will be closed for each of four phases.
Elevator Retrofitting	9/00	2 Months	Two (out of six) elevators will be shut down partially or fully during entire process.
Kitchen Upgrade and Expansion	12/01	2 Months	Some need to bring in external meals.
OB Unit Renovation and Expansion (Including Nursery)	6/00	24 Months	Loss of 25% to 50% of birthing, nursery and postpartum capacity at various periods.
Entryway Landscaping	3/02	1 Month	Limited pathways to front door from parking decks.
Build New Surgery Suite with Dedicated Same-Day Surgical Suites	3/01	18 Months	Minimal operational impact as operating room will be add-on construction; internal roadway detours.
Emergency Department Renovation and Expansion (with Fast Track and Imaging)	9/01	14 Months	Loss of 25 parking spaces, limited waiting space, loss of 10% to 20% of treatment rooms.

Key Observations

- **The objective of the overall renovation effort is to improve the viability of Bayshore for patient, physician and visitor access. For a period of 30 to 36 months, however, there will be a series of significant disruptions to physical access and way-finding, capacity and atmosphere.**

- **Two major clinical areas (OB and Emergency) will have capacity limitations that may cause loss of patient volume.**

■ DEFINING A MARKET POSITION

■ What Is Market Position?

A market position is a statement of where your product or service (or organization) is placed in the minds of the key audiences (usually the general public). Establishing a position is not something that an entity can do to itself. It is something that is done in the minds of the desired audiences. Organization leaders can work to change or secure a position by their actions, but, in the end, only the audiences can determine that entity A is in position X.

To put it another way, the leadership of St. Gerald Medical Center cannot get up one morning and announce to the world that St. Gerald is the "best" hospital on the west side of town. If St. Gerald truly does "own" this position or if the market is muddled enough that St. Gerald could make a claim to this position in the near future, then the leadership can take the actions needed to get consumers to formulate beliefs that St. Gerald is "best." This might involve facility improvements, new physicians, new services and various other strategies and actions.

Most entities never achieve a distinct market position. In and of itself, this is not necessarily a bad thing, but it does create a marketing challenge. Without some concept of a current or desired market position, it is very difficult for any organization to focus its marketing strategies and, in turn, its marketing actions. Moreover, without a distinct market position (one that is clearly recognized by the desired audiences), it is very unlikely that an organization will achieve a "brand" status.

■ Oh, You Mean 'Brand' Don't You?

No, I don't. As noted above, this workbook is not designed to go into great depth on the theory of marketing, but it is important to indicate that position and brand are not the same (though there is, of course, a relationship).

Here are a few brief observations on the issue of "brand" and "branding." For more, I would urge you to consult the myriad of books written on this topic.

- Brand or branding does not refer to your name, logo, signs, colors, etc. (unless you happen to be a cow). There are many in the marketing field (and not just in healthcare) who confuse identity with brand. Clearly, having a distinct identity is an important step on the road to becoming a brand, but creating a solid graphics standard and signage system does not make your entity into a brand.

- A brand is an organization, product or service that engenders an emotional attachment in a segment of the customer population that goes beyond the logic of objective factors such as access or price. To illustrate:

- We probably all know someone who will only drive a Ford or a Honda or a Cadillac. No amount of logic, price differentials or **Consumer Reports** guides will get them to change their preference. For these people, "Ford," etc., are brands.

- When I grew up in the New York City area, it was unthinkable for my mother (or anyone else in our known family/friend circle) to have any mayonnaise in the refrigerator other than "Hellman's." The attachment was emotional—her mother had used Hellman's, her friends used Hellman's—in fact, she had never tasted any other maker's product. For my mother (and my family) Hellman's is a brand.

- Time for a healthcare example—and one that illustrates that brands don't have to be limited to national entities or products. In my area there is an eight-physician pediatric practice that can trace its roots back to the 1950s. The practice has two offices and offers evening, Saturday and (believe it or not) Sunday hours. The practice has a knack for hiring warm, empathic staff and for bringing on the types of physicians whom kids and parents really like. In this immediate area (three to four zip codes), pediatric group X is a "brand."

The bottom line is that an organization or service does not have to have a distinct market position to be viable (or even successful). The lack of such a market position, however, makes the job of marketing the organization or service much more difficult because there is a lack of any specific direction or focus for the marketing efforts. There are many instances of healthcare entities that lack definitive market positions yet compete well in the area they serve. In my experience, however, far more often than not, the entities that lack any definitive market position are the ones that are more likely to lose the loyalty of various customer segments and thus close or be sold or become absorbed by another organization.

■ What Are the Important Characteristics of a Market Position?

Here are a few important characteristics of a market position:

- ***The market position must be credible, both internally and externally.*** I call this the "huh?" factor. If you claim a position in the market and the members of your key audiences (both internal and external) go "huh—I don't think so," the position is not credible. Sticking with this position will only serve to create a mental disconnect with those audiences. Consider the following examples:

▷ A 150-bed community hospital within 15 minutes drive of a nationally known research and teaching medical center attempts to stake a claim to the "best clinical care" in the specific market. Ads proclaiming leadership in a number of clinical specialties are greeted with strong skepticism by most area consumers.

▷ A 600-bed university facility attempts to stake a claim to a combination of "best care" and "convenient." The convenient claim is publicly derided by employees of the organization who live daily with inadequate parking, crowded waiting areas and three- to four-hour ER waits.

- *The market position must be unique within the defined market area.* One of the keys to a viable market position is to be unique in your industry segment in your geographic market. With few exceptions, most healthcare organizations do not have to worry about a national geographic scope—one city, metropolitan area or region is more than enough. To illustrate this point, look at the case study for Uptown University Medical Center. Uptown would probably achieve a solid level of consumer mental disconnect if it claimed a "best clinical care" position at a national level (in the face of the Johns Hopkins, Mayo Clinics, and others). It probably could, however, secure the "best clinical care" claim for the metropolitan area in which it is based and perhaps for another 50 to 100 miles around that area.

- *The market position must be reasonably defensible.* In other words, it should be a position that cannot be easily copied, bought or stolen by a competitor. Along those lines, market positions based on culture are generally more defensible than positions based on assets. Thus, a provider position based on being the leader relative to service quality is likely to be more defensible than a position based on having the leading technology. An atmosphere of top-notch personal service is a cultural situation built over a number of years. Having the leading technology can be matched by any competitor with enough resources to buy the technology. The following example illustrates the last point:

- Hospital A and hospital B are the two leading acute care providers in a county that contains five hospitals. The entities are essentially neck-and-neck relative to size, volumes and public awareness. Hospital A, however, has the area's only open-heart surgery program and thus has developed a market position as the "heart" hospital. In a 12-month period, hospital B upgrades its cardiac catheterization lab, expands its cardiac rehabilitation facility, doubles the scope of its heart-related education classes and educational ads, hires a top-quality cardiac surgery group and renovates two ORs for an open-heart surgery program. Within 24 months, hospital B takes nearly 40% of the open-heart case load and surpasses hospital A in terms of total cath volume.

Hospital B has not fully "stolen" hospital A's market position, but it has successfully muddled the picture to the point that hospital A no longer has a clear market position—and no specific focus to its marketing efforts. Hospital A had a position based largely on "assets"—one that was not overly defensible.

- *Market positions can change—but not frequently.* Once a position is defined and accepted and strategies are set in place to support/secure the position, you are committed. It is unwise, impractical and downright harmful to change the market position with each update of the marketing plan. Doing this creates confusion among members of your key audiences—and eventually results in having no position at all. Clearly, however, the world does change for all markets and all organizations. Over time (years, if not decades) the market position of an organization can change. It can be just as harmful to stick with an outdated position as it is to change positions every planning cycle. Here is an example of how a market position can change:

    ▷ Brookview Memorial is a 280-bed general acute care hospital located on the north side of a major city. In the 1950s through the early 1980s, Brookview was the "baby factory" for this part of the city. In fact, many of the people living in the neighborhoods around Brookview were born at the hospital. The OB niche position was well established in the consumer mindset. In the mid-1980s, increasing competition and a decline in the number of active obstetricians at Brookview began to take its toll. By the mid-1990s, Brookview was down to 500 deliveries per year with one active six-member OB group. At the same time, however, the organization was witnessing a steady increase in geriatric-oriented healthcare services. The "niche" position had changed, from OB to Senior Health/Geriatrics. With the realization and acceptance of this change, Brookview began to shift its internal and external marketing focus.

- *A market position is not your advertising tagline.* Your HMO may own the niche position of lowest premiums (cheapest). Your medical group may own the niche position of being the most convenient due to hours and locations. Your hospital may own the position of being high touch or caring in contrast to (against) the cold, impersonal teaching medical center. It is not advisable, however, to take these market positions and make them (verbatim) into your advertising taglines.

- *Warning! Everyone wants to be "best."* It must be human nature—everyone wants to be the "best." Whenever I recommend a market position other than a best position, I know that I will be in for some degree of battle with the leadership of the organization in question. The key is to remember that it is better to be unique in the minds of the consumer than it is to be noncredible and/or be part of a muddled mess of six entities all claiming some form of "best."

■ Do You Have Some Examples of Market Positions?

Here are a few nonhealthcare examples to illustrate the definitions of market position.

Position	Organization	Illustration of the Position
Best	BMW®	The best engineered cars
First	Coca-Cola®	The first/original cola
Against	Avis®	In contrast to the #1 supplier, they try harder to please customers.
Niche	Lifetime Television®	TV programming oriented toward women.
Combination	Jaguar®	Best within the luxury niche of cars

These are registered trademarks of BMW AG, the Coca-Cola Company, Avis Rent A Car System, Inc., Lifetime Entertainment Services, and Jaguar Cars North America, respectively.

Healthcare examples are not always so clear-cut, but the following should serve to illustrate the point.

Position	Organization	Illustration of the Position
Best Clinical—National	Johns Hopkins, Mayo Clinic	International reputations for cutting-edge medical capabilities
Best Clinical—Local Market	University hospital in a metro area with eight general hospitals	University offers the best capabilities in the local market.
Best Care—Local Market	Large pediatric group with four offices, late night and weekend services. Only group with pediatric subspecialists	Best range of services and best access
First	Not relevant for healthcare providers	
Against	Small acute care hospital competing with a tertiary teaching center	Hospital A is "against" (in contrast to) the cold, impersonal care offered by major medical center X.
Niche	Acute care hospital with only open heart capability in area	The "heart hospital" for county X
Niche	Physician group owns a chain of urgent care centers.	Niche of easy access to care
Combination	Religious acute care hospital is also the capability leader for cardiac care.	Combination of against and niche

Note the argument that "first" is not overly relevant in a healthcare setting. We hear this all the time—we had the first MRI in town, we are the first to do procedure X, we had the first pediatric ICU. What these individuals and entities really mean, however, is that we have the most experience because we have been at it the longest (in our area). This translates to a variation on a "best" position. For some consumers, being the "first" in the market also means having the oldest (least modern) equipment and technology! At best, a "first" position is short-lived for healthcare entities and must be converted to a "best" position in a fairly short time.

What about our case studies? Here are some possibilities:

- *High Plains HMO.* All of the available information indicates that High Plains is a borderline "commodity" with the other HMOs in the area. Premium rates are very close and the range of plan options is very similar. The one differentiating factor is that High Plains is owned by a provider organization. Thus a possible position for High Plains is a "niche" of being the provider-owned plan.

- *Uptown University Medical Center.* In light of what we know about Uptown, this organization should probably work with the market position of "best" or more likely "best clinical care" in the metropolitan area that it serves. In fact, no other position makes sense in light of Uptown's clear superiority in terms of range of services and clinical capabilities. "Best" may be a stretch for Uptown because while it is seen as the clinical leader, it is also seen as being a bit big, confusing, impersonal and a little below the norm for basic comfort and friendliness.

- *Bayshore Hospital.* This organization has a dominant market share and it is steadily improving its capabilities and facilities. It is also a very active participant in local civic, health, sporting and charitable events. On the other hand, the continued availability of more tertiary capabilities about an hour away limits this entity's ability to make claims to a clinical "best" position. This is a challenging case, but the market position of "best community provider" or "best local provider" is probably the most viable fit.

- *Wolfe Memorial Hospital.* The key factors for Wolfe are convenience and a solid reputation for warm, personal service. The hospital provides a fairly good level of quality for its range of capabilities, but no one is going to be fooled into thinking this is a tertiary center. The appropriate position for Wolfe may be a combination of "niche" and "against"—the convenient, caring facility in contrast to the more difficult to access and more impersonal medical centers in the city.

- *Polaris Occupational Health.* What we have learned is that no other provider of occupational health services can offer the range of services, professional expertise or geographic coverage that Polaris can offer. This leads to a possible market position of "best source."

■ Determining Market Strategies

■ What Is a Market Strategy?

A market strategy is a general "path" that the organization wishes to follow in order to meet a perceived opportunity or threat in the environment and/or support/secure the desired market position. It is a general statement, perhaps two or three sentences long. For example, St. Gerald Medical Center has joined forces with 200 of its physicians to form a risk-bearing PHO. The PHO has successfully negotiated contracts with two local commercial plans and two local Medicare risk plans. These four contracts offer the potential of up to 25,000 enrollees—but this is only a potential. The organization (along with two other PHOs and an IPA) still has to attract enrollees or convert them from their own patient panels. Thus, a potential market strategy for St. Gerald is as follows:

"Provide support to the development of enrollment by the St. Gerald PHO."

■ How Does a Strategy Differ from an Action or Tactic?

A market strategy essentially defines *what* you want to accomplish with your marketing efforts. An action (or tactic) defines *how* you are going to do it. Let's look at the strategy example shown above. "Provide support to the development of enrollment by the PHO" sets a path for what the organization wants to accomplish—but there is quite a long list of "how" that path might be followed. The following are some potential actions that might fall under this strategy:

- Develop a printed physician profile directory for distribution to potential enrollees.
- Sponsor open houses at the PCP office sites.
- Produce and place open-enrollment print ads in local newspapers.
- Develop interactive physician profiles on the PHO Web page, along with on-line enrollment forms.

Each of these potential actions will have specific implementation steps, time frames, resource requirements and responsible parties.

■ How Many Are Enough?

As with virtually every other part of a marketing plan, there is no magic number. Ideally, you want to have enough strategies to drive a reasonable amount of activity during the upcoming year. In turn, you don't want to have so many that the organization is paralyzed from the sheer volume. I recommend the following parameters:

- Medical group—four to six
- Small hospital—four to eight
- Large hospital/integrated system—six to twelve
- HMO—four to eight

■ Do You Have Any Examples?

The best way to illustrate the point about market strategies is to use the case studies discussed earlier in the book and some of the findings developed in their respective market audits. Here are some examples:

High Plains HMO

"Enhance open enrollment/employee conversion activities with client employers who offer a choice of health plans to their employees."

- This comes from an analysis of enrollment capture that shows High Plains has a declining percentage of employees who enroll with the plan in situations where there is a choice of plans.

"Develop cooperative marketing efforts with contracted PHO and IPA entities aimed at potential Medicare enrollees."

- High Plains has entered the Medicare risk market in the past 18 months and has negotiated with a number of PHO and IPA entities outside of its core provider unit service area. Experience in other markets shows that cooperative marketing efforts are best in terms of recruiting senior enrollees.

Uptown University Medical Center

"Improve the overall access to the Uptown campus with a special emphasis on way-finding to high-volume areas such as physician offices, outpatient clinics and testing services."

- The Uptown campus is universally recognized as a difficult site to navigate, especially for first-time or infrequent visitors. Employees routinely have to stop to direct patients and other visitors and there is a consistent pattern of lateness for tests and procedures due to difficulty in finding the appropriate office. Within the past year, two competitive, focused factory sites (facilities that focus on a particular clinical service) have opened within a mile of the campus and both have included easy access as one of the key selling points.

"Expand the internal and external scope of the medical call center as the key information and telephone access source for key audiences—consumers, patients and referring physicians."

- Uptown has a large medical call center operation that provides physician and service referral, nurse triage, physician after-hours coverage for 15 members of the staff, and referring physician to faculty physician contact. The center currently handles 90,000 calls per year, but this is projected as only one-third of the potential. A number of departments still handle their own incoming information calls (in inconsistent ways and with no computer support).

St. Gerald Medical Center

"Provide support for the development of enrollment by the St. Gerald PHO."

- St. Gerald's PHO has recently negotiated four risk contracts, giving the organization access to 25,000 lives. Assignment of lives is not guaranteed, however, and the PHO must compete with other PHOs and IPAs in the market for member enrollment.

"Restructure and enhance ongoing, postcontractual working relations with local managed care organizations."

- Recent research shows that the local managed care plans (over 15 in number) generally consider St. Gerald to be a difficult organization to work with. Some have openly observed that managed care operations at St. Gerald are "haphazard and confused." Responsibility for ongoing relations with managed care plans rests with five or six different internal functions. (This is an example of a strategy that is outside the normal range of a "marketing" department, but is still a major marketing issue for the organization as a whole.)

Bayshore Hospital

"Expand the Bayshore awareness, preference, image and provider presence in the northern portion of the primary and secondary service areas (four contiguous zip codes)."

- The northern portion of the PSA and the SSA is the area showing the most significant growth in population (projected at up to 3% per year for the next five years). There are four mid-size to large subdivisions in development, with three more in the application process. A large strip mall in the area is planning to expand and become enclosed. This area is currently served directly by only six active members of the Bayshore staff and it is the closest geographically to the tertiary competitor (45 to 60 minutes drive time from Bayshore, but only 30 minutes from the core of the north area).

"Maintain current levels of preference, image and volume for the OB program during the projected 24-month period of facility renovations and expansions."

- The campus renovation project, which will begin in October, will take 24 months to complete. The project includes a number of areas, but the focal point is a totally redone OB and nursery area. Construction will, at times, limit the number of available labor/delivery/recovery (LDR) rooms and other rooms. It will also make the environment less than ideal for a calm, quiet stay.

Wolfe Memorial Hospital

"Continue and expand community involvement activities (such as events, sponsorships, screenings, presentations and community group support) in the PSA and key parts of the SSA."

- Wolfe Memorial currently participates in a number of community events (but by far not all). It has a modest schedule of screenings, sponsorships and related activities. The two tertiary centers in the local city have begun to show up at some local events. Being local and being a part of the local community is one of the few competitive advantages that Wolfe has over the tertiary centers. For this reason, Wolfe needs to significantly step up its involvement with community groups and events.

"Enhance the marketing systems needed to support implementation of the position and strategies over the long term."

- Marketing functions at Wolfe have historically received little support, and many basic programs and standards (such as current collaterals, newcomer contact program, physician referral service and patient satisfaction tracking system) do not exist.

Central Valley Cardiology Associates

"Increase the number of physician referral sources regularly (defined as one referral every two months) sending patients to CVCA."

- Information shows that not only is the number of referrals declining, but so also is the number of referral sources. CVCA is becoming too reliant on a small group of referring physicians.

"Develop a process to track patient satisfaction with the experience and care received at CVCA offices."

- CVCA currently lacks any system to track patient satisfaction with the care received. Input from local HMO plans indicates some patient dissatisfaction with wait times to get appointments. (This is an example of a strategy that will likely be rephrased directly as the specific action.)

Polaris Occupational Health

"Expand the scope of available after-hours (night, weekend) occupational health services in submarkets where demand is likely to support the service."

- Polaris currently offers after-hours services only at its downtown location. Two smaller competitors recently added evening and limited weekend hours and there has been some anecdotal demand by clients for access beyond routine business periods.

"Establish a comparative price position for highly shopped occupational health services that is consistently 5% to 10% higher than local competitors."

- Internal and sales records show that employers routinely shop certain services such as drug screening and pre-employment physicals. The recent survey of area employers indicates that Polaris has a reputation and perceived level of quality that is 10% to 20% greater than any other competitor.

Setting Quantifiable Market Objectives

What Is a Market Objective?

A market objective is simply that factor (or factors) that we are going to aim for and measure to determine if we achieved anything as a result of the marketing plan.

What Are the Parameters of a Market Objective?

There are four important parameters to be used in setting market objectives for a marketing plan:

- *They need to be reasonable.* The objective should not be set so high or so far from the current state that achieving it is doomed from the start. For example, Wolfe Memorial has an OB market share in its PSA of 35%. By way of reference, a share point of OB in the Wolfe PSA is equal to 22 deliveries. There are plans under way to recruit a new OB/GYN physician, along with plans for a promotional campaign and other efforts. An objective of reaching a share level of 38% to 40% might be reasonable for the next year. An objective of reaching a share level of 65% in the next year is not.

- *They need to be challenging.* The objective should not be set so low that it would happen by osmosis. For example, High Plains has a market share of firms of 50+ employees of 39.3%. For the next year, it sets a goal of reaching a share of 39.4%. This is not much of a stretch. Unless the desired objective is to hold even, a bit more of a marketing challenge is probably in order.

- *They don't necessarily have to go up.* There is a tendency in developing a marketing plan to have every measurement go up. There is, of course, a natural endpoint to this pattern—and no organization that I know of has 100% market share, 100% preference share, or 100% patient satisfaction scores. Sometimes, it is a great marketing victory to hold onto what the organization already has. A PHO that has 80% of the capitated enrollment in the market has a far greater range to go down than to go up. A hospital that is about to renovate its emergency department will be lucky to keep the share that it has during the construction period.

- *They need to be quantifiable.* Over the years, marketing has taken a serious (and often justified) hit from other areas of healthcare management over its relative "worth." As accountability becomes more and more important, there is a need to quantify the objectives set for marketing.

■ Is an Objective the Same as a Goal?

To a minor degree, this is an example of "how many angels can dance on the head of a pin." By "traditional" planning standards (often used in strategic planning efforts), goals are statements of broad intent while objectives are the specific targets for the next year or finite short period. Some would consider the strategies noted above as goals. Others would use the word "goal" in place of the "objective" term used here. The reality is that it does not matter what terminology is used as long as the terms are commonly understood within the organization and used consistently over time. If you wish to call the quantifiable target measures goals instead of objectives, feel free to do so—just don't change the terminology with the next annual update of the marketing plan.

■ Does Every Objective Have To Be 'Quantified?'

No they don't, but the nonquantified objectives should be very rare indeed. If you opt to have any nonquantified objectives, make sure the leadership that will eventually judge the success or failure of the plan understands and accepts the objective.

■ Okay, Show Me What You Mean

Here are four objectives lifted from the pages of a number of recent marketing plans:

- Objective A—Increase referrals from PCPs based in Orange County.

- Objective B—Increase PHO enrollees from the senior 65+ plan.

- Objective C—Maintain OB market share in the face of major renovation efforts.

- Objective D—Increase top-of-mind awareness in the secondary service area north.

As you can see, none of these objectives has any quantification and thus no way to determine if anything has really been accomplished. If the number of referrals from PCPs in Orange County goes from 250 to 251, the organization has technically met the objective. In reality, however, nothing has been gained. Interestingly, all four can be quantified, as shown below:

- Objective A—Increase referrals from PCPs based in Orange County from 250 in the base year to 400 in CY 200A.

- Objective B—Increase senior 65+ enrollees from a base of 0 to 1,000 by the end of CY 200A.

- Objective C—Maintain OB market share at 45% during the 24-month construction period.

- Objective D—Increase top-of-mind awareness in the secondary service area north from 30% in the base year to 40% by CY 200B (the next projected consumer survey).

How Many Objectives Should We Have?

Once again, there is no magic number. Ideally, there should be enough to generate some reasonable level of tracking of results, but not so many that the marketing staff spends inordinate numbers of hours updating measurements. For example, an objective of top-of-mind awareness for the entire nine-zip-code PSA is probably a good idea, while a top-of-mind objective for each zip code within the PSA is probably overkill. A medical group or specialty service or program might have four to six objectives for a year. A smaller hospital might have six to 10 objectives. A larger hospital or diversified system might have up to 25 to 30 objectives including subobjectives for service lines or geographic sectors.

Do You Have Any Examples?

Here are some commonly used objectives for healthcare provider organizations. This is by no means an end-all list, but most organizations can use some of these objectives.

- Volumes—admissions, visits, surgeries, tests
- Market share
- Number or share of capitated lives
- Number of employer contracts (HMO or occupational medicine)
- Telephone inquiries for physician referral
- Sales calls made
- Reenrollment levels
- Patient satisfaction scores
- Number of referrals
- Number of referral sources
- Number of members (senior groups, fitness centers)
- Special event participation
- Number of participants in classes or screenings
- Top-of-mind awareness
- Preference scores
- Image ratings

How Does It Look?

The following is a summary table of market objectives for St. Gerald Medical Center. Each objective has a baseline measure, a desired level for the next year CY 200A and an initial desired level for the year after that (CY 200B). Since many hospital-based objectives are similar regardless of the organization's size, St. Gerald will stand as a proxy for Uptown University, Bayshore and Wolfe. Following this table are some possible objectives for nonhospital entities such as High Plains, Central Valley and Polaris.

Measurement	Base Year (1)	CY 200A	CY 200B
Market Share			
Inpatient Share – PSA (2)	31.5%	32.5%	34.0%
Inpatient Share – SSA North (2)	14.4%	16.0%	18.0%
Inpatient Share – SSA South (2)	8.5%	9.0%	9.0%
Emergency Share – PSA (3)	50%	50%	50%
Emergency Share – SSA North (3)	16%	18%	21%
Emergency Share – SSA South (3)	6%	6%	6%
Outpatient Surgery Share – PSA (3)	48%	50%	54%
Outpatient Surgery Share – SSA North (3)	21%	24%	27%
Outpatient Surgery Share – SSA South (3)	10%	10%	10%
Patient Satisfaction			
Overall Inpatient Score (4)	84.5	85.0	86.0
Overall Emergency Department Score (4)	78.0	80.0	82.0
Overall Outpatient Surgery Score (4)	88.4	88.0	88.0
Overall Outpatient Score (4)	86.0	88.0	88.0
Preference Share			
Inpatient Preference – PSA (3)	35%	38%	42%
Emergency Dept. Preference – PSA (3)	47%	47%	47%
Outpatient Surgery Preference – PSA (3)	51%	53%	55%
Note: Repeated for Both SSAs			
OB Preference – Total Area (3)	45%	48%	52%
Cardiology Preference – Total Area (3)	40%	45%	50%
Oncology Preference – Total Area (3)	35%	35%	35%
Top-of-Mind Awareness			
Primary Service Area (3)	56%	60%	65%
Secondary Service Area North (3)	26%	30%	35%
Secondary Service Area South (3)	15%	15%	15%
Other			
Image Rating (3)	3.10	3.25	3.40
Rated "Best Hospital" (3)	45%	50%	55%
Community Event Participation (5)	7,200	8,000	9,000
Wellness Center Memberships (6)	0	1,100	2,500
PHO Enrollment (7)	1,500	3,500	6,000

(1) Base Year for each objective measurement:
- For inpatient share—CY 1998
- For emergency department and outpatient surgery share—CY 1999
- For patient satisfaction—July 1998 to June 1999
- For preference share—CY 1999
- For top-of-mind awareness—CY 1999
- For image rating—CY 1999
- For rated "best hospital"—CY 1999
- For community event participation—CY 1998
- For Wellness Center memberships—June 1999
- For PHO enrollment—June 1999

(2) Source: State Hospital Association database

(3) Source: 1999 St. Gerald consumer survey. Image rating score is based on a 1 to 4 scale, with 1 = poor, 2 = fair, 3 = good, and 4 = excellent. Preference rating for OB, cardiology and oncology represents both PSA and SSA.

(4) Source: St. Gerald patient satisfaction survey system. Base year represents the average of four quarters of ratings. Top score = 100.

(5) Source: Marketing and Education Department internal records on event and class participation.

(6) Source: St. Gerald Wellness Center records of paid membership. Center to open September 1999.

(7) Source: PHO internal records of membership.

High Plains HMO

Measurement	Base Year	CY 200A	CY 200B
Qualified Leads – Advertising Campaign	125	150	200
Capture Rate – Employees	43.2%	44.0%	45.0%

Central Valley Cardiology Group

Measurement	Base Year	CY 200A	CY 200B
Active Referral Sources	35	38	42
Cardiology Capitated Lives	0	1,000	2,000

Polaris Occupational Health

Measurement	Base Year	CY 200A	CY 200B
Pre-Employment Physicals	4,500	4,800	5,500
Health Back Program Paid Participants	500	600	750

Defining Market Actions

What Is a Market Action?

The market actions are the "nuts and bolts" of the marketing plan. This is where you lay out what the organization will actually do in the upcoming year relative to marketing activities.

It is important to note that the market actions are ideally no more than one or two pages long. Anything longer than this is getting into too much detail. Remember that you may have 20, 30 or more actions. It will take some time to think out and write up these actions without creating a volume the size of a long novel. Moreover, the details that you think up today will likely change by the time you implement the action three, six or more months from now. The ultimate objective is to develop a viable marketing plan and then act on it—not to spend your career writing planning documents.

But What About My Advertising Campaign or Physician Recruitment Plan?

The details of the projected advertising campaign are not likely to be developed until several months after the marketing plan is done. The marketing plan needs to be completed so you can get to what really counts—implementation. Limit the description of a major action that requires its own planning and documentation to one or two pages and save the details (such as campaign concept, design and media plan) for an appendix or subsequent document.

Are These Marketing Department Actions or Organizational Actions?

If all of the market actions are assigned to the marketing staff for responsibility, you have essentially created a marketing department work plan, not an organizational marketing plan. There is nothing inherently wrong with the first approach, but it will not result in the creation of a marketing-oriented culture within your entity.

Ideally, the marketing plan should be organizationwide in scope. The reality is that much of the focus will be on "traditional" activities (such as advertising and events) and much of the work will be done by the designated marketing staff—but not all of it. Some of the actions should involve program development, key audience relations, sales, and even pricing and facility issues. Some of the actions should have the responsibility assigned to line managers, operational vice presidents, and even the CFO and the CEO. Needless to say, these individuals should be involved in the development of the actions for which they will be responsible.

■ Do We List Every Activity Done Under 'Marketing?'

No. The market actions should be limited to activities that are either new or require distinctly noticeable levels of effort or resources. The routine functions of a marketing department would not require specific market action statements.

The following types of activities would likely result in distinct market action write-ups:

- An advertising campaign to support the newly renovated OB unit
- The patient satisfaction tracking process
- The medical staff newsletter
- Development of a new PCP practice on the south side of the PSA
- A relationship management program aimed at area employers
- Expansion of the call center to handle referring physician to faculty physician contacts
- Expansion of the Web page to handle ancillary testing scheduling

The following types of activities would probably not result in distinct market action write-ups:

- Routine responses to press inquiries or routine press releases
- Attendance at ongoing management meetings
- Restocking brochure distribution points
- Photographing visiting VIPs

■ Do All of the Marketing Actions Have To Be New?

Absolutely not. It will vary by organization and by what is happening in the local market, but in a given year perhaps only one-quarter to one-third of the actions will be new. The balance will be continuations (perhaps with some adjustments) of distinct marketing activities that are still valuable to the entity. For example, Polaris Occupational Health conducts a series of "Business Breakfasts" three to four times per year. These have been going on for a few years and always have a good attendance and good returns for Polaris in terms of contacts. This is an ongoing activity that will be included as a distinct market action in the Polaris marketing plan.

■ Is There Any Special Way That Market Actions Should Be Labeled?

On the surface this seems like a fairly straightforward issue, yet amazingly I have seen internal battles over how actions should be labeled. The answer is simple—pick a method that is easy to use, makes some degree of logical sense and is consistent over time. If there is a system that already exists in the organization's strategic plan or other accepted document, copy it. Call them actions 1, 2, 3, etc., as high as you need to go. Call them actions A, B, C, etc. (of course this limits you to 26 unless you like AA, AB, etc.). Call them 1-1, 3-2, etc. (for strategy 1, action 1 or strategy 3, action 2). The limitation here, as noted earlier, is that one action may not fit neatly under one strategy. Call them Tom, Dick and George. Enough already—call me a cab.

■ Do the Market Actions Have To Fit Under Specific Market Strategies?

This is another one of those issues that really doesn't matter in the end, but often causes a lot of internal debate. My experience and opinion is that if you really want to "force" each market action to fit under a specific market strategy, go ahead and do it that way. There is nothing wrong with this approach, but there is nothing excessively right about it either. It can be argued that a particular market action could support two or three different market strategies. If this happens, how should the labeling work? Sometimes it is just easier to not force the issue and to simply note that this action supports strategies 2, 4 and 7.

An alternative is to group the market actions into logical categories such as communications, community events/education, medical staff activities, new programs and so forth.

■ What Is Included in a Market Action?

There are seven primary components (and two optional components) of a market action, as follows:

- *Strategy* (Optional). Which market strategy does the market action fall under?

- *Description.* A brief write-up describing what the market action is about. Usually three or four sentences is sufficient, perhaps a bit more for a new action that will be unfamiliar to those reading the marketing plan.

- *Implementation steps.* A brief listing of the major steps that need to be taken in order to implement this specific market action. A typical action will have 5 to 10 such steps listed, with usually no more than one or two sentences in each step.

    It is important to note that the implementation steps should be reasonably broad in nature. For example, one logical step for a publication could be:

    "Distribute the XYZ Newsletter to the target audience."

    It is *not* necessary to take this to the level of:

    "Get the newsletters from the printer."
    "Apply labels."

"Apply appropriate postage."

"Take newsletters to the Post Office."

- ***Rationale.*** This is essentially a brief description of why you are even bothering with this specific market action. If you cannot come up with a reasonable rationale for the action, you need to question why the organization is even bothering to do it. Ideally, the rationale should connect back to one of the key observations in the market audit (or to the fact that this is a successful, ongoing effort or to the political fact that the leadership wants it to happen). Again, two or three sentences should be sufficient to describe the rationale.

- ***Priority level.*** What is the priority level for this action? (See the section on setting priorities, page 67.)

- ***Time frame.*** This refers to when the action is anticipated to begin, not how long it will take. Usually a month/year time frame (March 2000 or June 2001) is sufficient. The exact date of beginning is not necessary and probably not accurate.

  In some instances, an action is ongoing throughout the entire year or ongoing with specific delivery points. These can be labeled that way. For example, the time frame for the patient satisfaction tracking system (which is mailed constantly and reported monthly) could be labeled as "ongoing." The time frame for a quarterly publication could be labeled as "ongoing" (issues in September 1999, January 2000, April 2000 and June 2000).

  The primary purpose of determining time frames/start dates is to establish an overall time view of the marketing plan and to eliminate potential logjams. If Uptown University ends up with 45 market actions in its marketing plan and 19 of them are tentatively targeted for April, then it may be appropriate to shift a few around to reduce the potential of a major logjam (or marketing function "crash").

- ***Resources required.*** Although every part of the market action write-up is important, this section is crucial for determining the budget needed to support the marketing activities. Development of the resources estimates should be done carefully and where possible, should be based on actual prior experience or input from external sources (such as consultants, the literature, or sister provider entities). There are three potential components of the resources section:

  ▷ Manpower
  ▷ Funding
  ▷ Other resources

  Each of these components is discussed in detail in the remainder of this section.

Manpower. Manpower is a factor of how much staff time is estimated to be needed to complete a specific market action over the course of the year time period for the marketing plan. Usually this staff time is expressed in a range, such as 50 to 75 hours or 150 to 200 hours. It includes the time from all members of the organization's staff, not just the marketing department staff. Some examples of these staff time estimates include:

▷ (Newcomer contact program.) Estimate 50 to 75 staff hours for development of creative materials. Estimate 75 to 100 staff hours to oversee ongoing distribution of the materials to new residents in the PSA and SSA.

▷ (Physician profiles for Web page.) Estimate 150 to 200 staff hours to develop profiles and add materials to St. Gerald's Web page.

▷ (Shopping mall-based health education center.) Estimate 250 to 300 staff hours to establish the center. Estimate 0.75 FTE to staff the center for the balance of the marketing plan year.

In all of the cases discussed above, the staff time shown is for all members of the organization involved in the market action, whether in the marketing department or other areas. In some cases, organizations prefer to split out the staff time directly from the marketing department from all other staff time, for example:

▷ (Shopping mall-based health education center.) Estimate 250 to 300 staff hours to establish the center (60% marketing). Estimate 0.75 FTE (10% marketing, balance between community education, Senior Advantage, nursing and administration) to staff the center for the balance of the marketing plan year.

The assumption is made in the resource requirements noted above that the manpower is coming from existing organizational staff. On occasion, a market action requires the addition of new manpower. This should be distinctly noted in the resources section, as illustrated below:

▷ (Expand medical call center to provide after-hours triage services for owned FP, IM, OB/GYN and pediatric practices.) Estimate 4.5 FTE RN staff time, of which 2.5 FTE will be new hires added to the call center.

Remember that 2,080 hours (or 2,000 hours for simplicity) is the same as one FTE. Thus, a market action that would require 500 to 600 staff hours could also be expressed as 0.25 to 0.30 FTE.

The estimation of staff hours for specific actions, especially new ones, is a combination of educated guesswork and experience. One methodology that can help reduce the guesswork over time is to establish a job coding system, similar to the ones used by most consulting firms or advertising agencies. Each action is assigned a job code and all staff record their time against each code on a daily basis. While this will not result in any billing, it will provide a more accurate picture as to how much time is really being spent on sales calls on employers, for example, or on the medical staff newsletter.

Funding. This refers to the actual dollar funding required to implement an action. Depending on the organization, the funding resource requirement should reflect the total cost required to fund the action for a year and the actual funds required for the portion of the plan year that the action will actually be in effect. Thus, a particular action may require $100,000 for one full year, but because it will not go into effect until six months into the year, the plan year funding is only $50,000. Some examples of funding estimates include:

▷ (MD office open houses joint venture with Senior HMO entity.) Estimate $25,000 for literature, materials, invitations, postage, and refreshments. This is for six planned open houses, representing the 50% cost share for Bayshore Hospital.

▷ (Monthly print ad to support St. Gerald community education programs.) Estimate $31,500 for ad template design, monthly camera-ready materials and ad placement for one year.

▷ (Social event meetings with top 20 referral sources.) Estimate $4,500 for meals and entertainment (tickets, etc.) for social meetings between senior partners of Central Valley Cardiology Associates and the top 20 referring physicians for the past 12 months.

Be careful in estimating funding for various actions, especially those not under the control of the function responsible for developing the marketing plan. Review historical records carefully and check industry standards to get reasonable measures. For example, participation in a series of industrial trade shows for Polaris Occupational Health involves the cost of a display, giveaway items and trade show fees. It could also involve the printing of additional literature to give to show visitors—a cost that would not have been incurred but for this action.

Sometimes a new action involves one-time costs to get the effort going. This should be acknowledged in the resources section. For example, starting a new publication aimed at area employers might involve a one-time cost in the design of the publication as well as ongoing costs for printing, lists, postage, mail handling and similar items.

Other Resources. This category is not seen all that often in marketing plans, but could include rental space, computers, capital equipment (a major trade show display, for example), a vehicle, etc.

- *Responsible Party.* One of the best ways to guarantee that a marketing plan will fail is to make sure that no one takes responsibility for implementation. The parties responsible for implementing each action should be noted right in the action write-ups. This means the key individuals responsible, not every staff member who might work on the activity. Thus an action calling for the development of package prices for elective surgical procedures might be assigned to the CFO, even though staff members from two or three areas might develop the prices.

  One issue that occasionally comes up is whether or not to identify positions or individual names. It really doesn't matter, as long as everyone understands who is being identified. My personal preference is for position titles, just in case people change jobs. Thus the identification of responsible parties could look like either of the following:

  ▷ Vice President of Marketing
  ▷ Director of Outpatient Surgery Services

  or

  ▷ Tom Smith (Vice President of Marketing)
  ▷ Mary Jones (Director of Outpatient Surgery Services)

- *Cross Reference* (Optional). On occasion, a marketing plan has a number of subcomponents, such as an organizationwide marketing plan with action subsets for four service lines (cardiology, women's and children's, oncology and neurosciences, for example). Each of the four service line subsets could call for an action related to getting lead physicians onto local television and radio shows. To avoid conflict and confusion, these actions should reference each other.

  Even in single entity plans, some degree of cross-referencing can occur. The promotion of a new urgent care site could call for a profile on the hospital's Web page, articles in the quarterly community publication and mentions on the drive-time radio health minute. Each of these are distinct market actions in their own right. A cross-reference could help to reduce confusion.

■ How Do You Set Priorities for Market Actions?

The establishment of priorities for market actions is somewhat artificial and often varies from organization to organization. The priority levels will be impacted by the perceived importance of various market strategies, the political, operational and budgetary needs of the organization and the ever-changing dictates of the market. If the organization believes that a strategy focusing on physician recruitment is essential, the two or three actions associated with that strategy will likely be considered as top priority. If there are some severe budget constraints due to the loss of a managed care contract, some additional actions may have to slip to a secondary priority level. If, in the middle of the year, a major competitor announces a new freestanding facility, promotion of your freestanding center may move up in priority.

The purpose of setting priorities for market actions is to focus organizational energies as efficiently as possible. Experience shows that if everything is a "top" priority, then essentially nothing is a priority—and often very little actually gets accomplished (or the staff burns out trying to accomplish everything).

Unless the organization is very large and/or very complex, two levels of priority are usually sufficient. By experience, they would include the following:

- *Priority one.* This consists of actions that are dictated by market circumstances or executive leadership to be essential to achieve the market position or to support significant organizational initiatives. This might also include actions that must be accomplished in order to allow the accomplishment of other key actions.

- *Priority two.* This comprises actions that would be useful and beneficial for the organization, but will not materially hinder the market position or key organization initiatives if not implemented in the upcoming year. Priority two actions are likely to become priority one actions the next year if they are not implemented.

While there is no absolute rule, most organizations end up with two-thirds to three-quarters of their market actions in the priority one category, with the balance being in the priority two category.

■ How Many Market Actions Should We Have?

Like anything in a marketing plan, there is no magic number. Ideally, there should be enough market actions in the upcoming year to challenge the organization and to go beyond the routine flow. On the other hand, there shouldn't be so many that the organization is paralyzed by inability to handle the load. Having said that, here are some possible guidelines:

- Medical group – 10 to 15
- Small hospital – 20 to 30
- Large hospital/integrated system – 30 to 50
- HMO – 20 to 30

We Have a Lot of Actions. Should We Have a Summary?

A one- or two-page summary of the market actions is a useful tool for a variety of purposes. It helps managers who don't have the time to read all of the market action write-ups. It serves as a quick checklist on the time frames and resources for actions. It also serves as a quick way to summarize the total resources required for the marketing plan. There are probably an infinite number of ways to create a summary table for market actions, but a format that seems to work well is the following.

Action	Description	Priority/Time Frame	Resources	Responsible
A-1	Continue community quarterly publication	One/March 200A	Estimate 150-200 staff hours and $75,000 for printing, list and postage	Director of Communications
A-2	Direct mail to support urgent care center	One/April 200A	Estimate 75-100 staff hours and $65,000 for design, production, list, postage	Director of Communications Vice President of Ambulatory Care
B-1	Update consumer survey	One/June 200A	Estimate 25-50 staff hours and $22,000 for research agency	Vice President of Planning
C-1	Develop Wellness Center pricing schedule	Two/September 200A	Estimate 15-25 staff hours	CFO Director of Wellness Center
Etc.				

■ How Does the Market Action Summary Lead to a Marketing Budget?

Take all of the funds estimated for the various first and second priority market actions. Subtract any of those funds that are assumed to be in divisions or departments other than the formal marketing department. Add in departmental salaries, supplies, memberships, travel and other miscellaneous line items and you have a marketing department budget for a full year. Leave in the funding allocations to other divisions or departments and you have an organizationwide marketing budget for a year.

This activity serves two purposes. First, it allows the marketing leadership to prepare a budget that is effectively zero-based; that is, built from the ground up to support the well-planned marketing direction of the organization. This is the desired way to set a budget, as opposed to the methods often found in healthcare organizations (such as "take last year's budget and add 3%" or "how much do we have left over from everything else?"). Second, it allows the organization to match marketing plans with financial reality. If the first priority market actions result in a funding estimate of $1,000,000 and the reality is that the marketing effort can only be funded up to a level of $700,000, it becomes clear fairly quickly that something needs to change. Some actions must drop to second priority, be cut back in scope or be dropped totally.

There is a parallel effort for manpower allocation. By adding up all of the hours and partial FTEs estimated for all of the first and second priority market actions, the organization can develop a fairly good picture of the manpower needed to support the annual marketing efforts. As a subset of this examination, look closely at the hours estimated for the marketing department. Add in the hours required for routine activities and the result is a good picture of the manpower needed for the marketing department for the upcoming year. If all of the first priority actions plus routine activity result in a need for 8.5 FTEs and the marketing department only has 5.0, something needs to change. There is a need to add staff, change some priorities or drop some actions.

■ Do You Have Some Examples?

It wouldn't be much of a book on marketing plans if I didn't. Here are some examples of market actions lifted from the pages of actual marketing plans developed in recent years (but assigned to the case studies used here).

Market Action Example One (St. Gerald)

Action 16 – Develop a Formal Publication for Area Employers

Strategy	*Strategy Six.* Target area employers for support and sale of services.
Action Description	Develop a quarterly publication aimed at area employers. This publication would focus on the services and personnel of St. Gerald, health issues in the local community and health issues in the workplace. The initial target audience for this publication will be senior executives in all firms in the PSA and SSA with 50 or more employees (estimated at 1,500). Consideration will be given to expansion to smaller employers in 2001. (Note: A potential alternative to a publication is a series of direct mail pieces. Impact and cost of both alternatives will be explored before a final determination is made.)
Implementation Steps	1. Develop a name and design for the publication. 2. If appropriate (pending design), print a one year supply of mastheads. 3. Develop an editorial calendar for the first four issues. 4. Secure sources of articles (both internal and external sources). 5. Obtain and maintain an appropriate mailing list. 6. Write, produce and print each issue. 7. Distribute by mail, using the contracted mail house. 8. Track all calls to action noted in the publication. 9. Add publication articles to a new section of the St. Gerald Web page.
Rationale	Interviews conducted among area employers indicate that these individuals have very limited familiarity with St. Gerald. Most noted that their only contact with the hospital is for occupational health sales or fundraising. In light of managed care and local political issues, increased familiarity and support among employers are desirable.
Priority	Two
Time Frame	September 200A
Resources	• Estimate 25 to 50 staff hours to design and produce the initial publication masthead. • Estimate 25 to 50 staff hours per issue (100 to 200 per year) for writing, production and distribution. • Estimate $8,000 for masthead design and initial printing. • Estimate $16,000 for the printing, list and postage for four issues.
Responsible	Assistant Vice President, Communications Director, Occupational Health Services

■ Market Action Example Two (Bayshore)

Action B-1 – Update the Consumer Survey

Strategy	*Strategy B.* Keep marketing systems and databases current.
Action Description	Update the biannual consumer survey. This survey covers the PSA and the northern and southern portions of the SSA.
Implementation Steps	1. Secure the services of an external research firm. (Note: Unless circumstances dictate otherwise, Bayshore will use the ABC Research Agency, the same firm that has conducted the last three consumer surveys.) 2. Solicit input from the Bayshore management team for changes, deletions and additions to the survey instrument. 3. Prepare the survey and field to the PSA and SSA. Unless circumstances dictate otherwise, maintain the sampling plan used for the past three survey efforts. 4. Obtain the raw survey results and work with the external agency to develop an analysis of the current situation and a comparison with prior findings. 5. Distribute the written report from the external agency to appropriate Bayshore managers and leaders. 6. Incorporate the survey findings into the annual market audit presentation to management and board.
Rationale	The information derived from the consumer survey is an important part of the input that goes into the development of the Bayshore marketing plan. It is also used to track the success of various marketing initiatives used by Bayshore.
Priority	One
Time Frame	May 200A
Resources	Estimate 25 to 50 staff hours to update the survey and to work with the research firm. $22,000 for survey implementation (using an external research firm).
Responsible	Vice President, Planning and Marketing

- **Market Action Example Three (Bayshore)**

Action D-1 Increase the Frequency of the *Around The Halls* Publication

Strategy	*Strategy D.* Internal communications improvements.
Action Description	Increase the frequency of the *Around The Halls* publication from its current rate of six times per year (bimonthly) to 24 times per year (biweekly). Reduce the size of the publication from 12 to 16 pages per issue to 4 to 6 pages per issue (unless information dissemination needs dictate additional length for specific issues). Continue current content but give priority to operating and personnel issues that impact the internal Bayshore family. Develop a simplified format that improves readability and reduces the production costs per issue.
Implementation Steps	1. Revise the format of the publication. 2. Develop an editorial calendar, outlining regular columns for each issue. 3. Enhance the system of providing input for the publication via selected reporters for each division and department. 4. Write, lay out and produce the publication on a biweekly basis. 5. Distribute via existing methods (internal drop points and mailings to physician offices).
Rationale	There is some indication (via survey and anecdotal input) that internal audiences believe information about organizational issues does not get to them in a timely manner. This problem is also highlighted by the large number of internal entitywide memos, broadcast e-mails and postings used to disseminate information.
Priority	One
Time Frame	Initiate new schedule in February 200A.
Resources	• Estimate 400 to 500 staff hours per year. • Estimate $5,000 per year for printing (done internally) and postage.
Responsible	Director, Public Relations Publications Coordinator

■ Market Action Example Four (Polaris Occupational Health)

Action 6 – Target Additional Employers for On-Site Medical Services

Strategy	*Strategy Four.* Expand business opportunities out of Polaris sites.
Action Description	Explore opportunities to develop and contract-manage additional on-site medical offices for area employers.
Implementation Steps	**Phase One** 1. Initiate contacts and negotiations with three qualified leads relative to on-site opportunities. 2. Prepare proposal packages with information responsive to specific questions, summary of experience at current site and pricing options. 3. Aim to secure one of the three qualified leads within 90 days of the initiation of negotiation efforts. Use pricing incentives if necessary to accomplish this goal. **Phase Two** 4. Pursue publicity (via local business publications and Polaris web page) for existing on-site contracts. 5. Develop sales support package using experience from existing contract sites. 6. Initiate sales contacts with target list firms. 7. Develop specific proposals and conduct appropriate negotiations based on feedback from target list firms. 8. Evaluate customer satisfaction, clinical results and financial return from on-site contracts on a quarterly basis.
Rationale	The initial experience developing and contract-managing an on-site medical office for XYZ Manufacturing has been a clinical and financial success since its inception 18 months ago. Three other firms have approached Polaris about similar efforts, and research indicates that the market has 25 firms of a size and industry type to potentially justify such an effort.
Priority	One
Time Frame	Initiate contacts with initial target list firms by May 200A.
Resources	• Estimate 25 to 50 hours to develop specialized sales support materials. • Estimate 75 to 100 hours to develop target list and make initial sales calls. • $5,000 for sales support materials. • Hours and costs for formal bid efforts to be determined.
Responsible	President Director, Sales

Market Action Example Five (High Plains HMO)

Action D-1 – Expand Postsales Conversion Capabilities

Strategy	*Strategy D.* Enrollment and conversion activities.
Action Description	Expand the number of staff available for postsales conversion of qualified employees. It is anticipated that this expansion will enable High Plains to participate in 20 additional work site events aimed at enrollment.
Implementation Steps	1. Finalize job descriptions for the new staff members. 2. Place advertisements in appropriate locations, including trade journals and local print media. 3. Place job openings on the employment section of the High Plains Web page. 4. Contact potential candidates identified during the recent hiring effort for High Plains sales staff and High Plains Hospital patient representatives. 5. Screen employment submissions and interview potential candidates. 6. If appropriate, select final candidates, make job offers and secure job acceptances. 7. Provide new hires with appropriate training on High Plains products and the enrollment process.
Rationale	Analysis conducted as part of the market audit shows a declining rate of employee conversion after the sale of a plan contract. Over the past two years, High Plains has been unable to support all open enrollment events requested or available from employers.
Priority	One
Time Frame	Initiate in May 200A to have new staff on board by beginning of the fiscal year (July 200A).
Resources	• Estimate 125 to 150 staff hours to support new hiring effort. • Add 3.0 new FTEs (budgeted at $135,000 for salaries and benefits). • $20,000 for computers, office equipment, training and travel costs.
Responsible	Director, Member Relations

Market Action Example Six (Central Valley Cardiology Associates)

Action 5 – Referral Source Satisfaction Tracking

Strategy	*Strategy One.* Referral source relations.
Action Description	Obtain input from referral sources on their satisfaction with the services provided by CVCA to their patients and the quality of the interaction between CVCA and their practice. Target all referral sources from the past year (N = 103).
	Part A – Senior practice partners will meet with the top 10 referring physicians by volume.
	Part B – A written survey will be sent to all other referral sources.
Implementation Steps	1. Finalize list of referral sources for prior year.
	2. Senior practice partners will target top 10 sources. Contact will be made personally to set a breakfast or lunch meeting.
	3. Develop an informal question/interview guide for top 10 meetings.
	4. Meet with top 10 referral sources and record feedback.
	5. Develop written survey and cover letter. (Use research support from the Hospital A marketing department.)
	6. Mail out survey to all remaining referral sources.
	7. Track responses and send second mailing to nonrespondents.
	8. Tabulate results and prepare a written report.
Rationale	Feedback on relations with referral sources is at best sporadic. Within the past year, CVCA has lost two referral sources due to perceived patient results feedback problems.
Priority	One
Time Frame	Initiate contacts and implement survey in October 200A.
Resources	• Estimate 40 to 50 staff hours for visits, survey design and tabulation of results.
	• $300 for meals with top referral sources.
	• Estimate less than $100 for postage for written survey.
Responsible	Senior Practice Partners (Drs. Smith and West)
	Executive Director

■ Market Action Example Seven (Polaris Occupational Health)

Action 11 – Participate in Local Business Trade Shows

Strategy	*Strategy Two*. Promote Polaris to generate qualified leads.
Action Description	Participate with a display booth in the Metropolitan Business Expo (April) and the Eastern Regional Manufacturers' Expo (October). (Note: Existing display has reached the end of its useful life and needs to be replaced.)
Implementation Steps	1. Research new display options and purchase a display appropriate for the budget and the shows in question. 2. Register for trade show space in a timely manner to secure prime locations. Arrange for electrical connections, shipping and setup/takedown assistance. 3. Prepare and submit trade show directory ads. 4. Select and purchase appropriate giveaway materials. 5. Secure the use of a popcorn-making machine and appropriate supplies. 6. Establish a trade show staffing schedule for Polaris sales, management and clinical staff (three people at all times in the booth).
Rationale	These two trade shows draw a combined 13,000 participants, largely from organizations and firms that represent the core clients for Polaris. Over the past five years, Polaris has averaged two new clients per show.
Priority	One
Time Frame	Targeted trade shows are in April and October 200A.
Resources	• Estimate 75 to 100 staff hours to prepare for and staff both shows. • $12,000 for a new display booth with shelves, photographs and related materials. • $3,500 for trade show entry fees, rental of a popcorn machine, electrical connections and setup/takedown labor. • $14,000 for giveaway materials, including prizes for business card drops.
Responsible	Director, Sales Director, Clinical Services

Market Action Example Eight (Uptown University Medical Center)

Action E-1 – Direct Contacts with Referring Physicians

Strategy	*Strategy Six.* Enhance relations with regional referral sources.
Action Description	Target referral sources in the PSA and SSA for active contact by members of the senior management team of Uptown University. The objectives of this effort are to address any hindrances to referrals by these sources and to encourage additional referrals to Uptown faculty physicians.
	Based on available information, there are 320 physicians in the PSA and 520 physicians in the SSA who referred a patient to Uptown faculty physicians or programs over the past 12 months. While the ultimate objective of this effort is to meet with all these physicians, the initial target for 200A will be 200 contacts (in a to-be-determined mix of referral volumes, specialties and geography).
	The referring physician contact effort will include the following senior managers: CEO; Executive VP; Senior VP, Medical Staff Affairs; Senior VP, Patient Services; Senior VP, Finance; VP, Planning and Marketing; VP, Nursing Services; VP, Ambulatory Care Services; VP, Operations; VP, Human Resources; Director of Marketing, Director of Planning, Director, Medical Staff Office.
Implementation Steps	1. Using existing referral records plus directories of physicians in the PSA and SSA, develop a list of potential visit candidates.
	2. Develop a game plan for visits for the first year. Suggested parameters include referral volume level, referral volume potential, geography and clinical areas targeted as priorities for promotion (cardiac services, neuroscience services).
	3. Use support staff to contact potential interviewees and schedule meetings.
	4. Develop an informal discussion/interview guide for use by all Uptown participants.
	5. Develop a high-quality packet of materials to support the meetings.
	6. Conduct one-on-one meetings with referral sources at a location of convenience to them (or at Uptown, if possible).
	7. Summarize any key inputs, requests and complaints. Record in the referral source database.
	8. Follow up on meetings with a formal written response.
Rationale	As a regional tertiary center, Uptown University relies on the referrals of primary care and community-based specialty physicians. Direct, two-way communication with these sources is essential to ensure that all systems support this referral process.
Priority	One
Time Frame	Initiate meetings by June 200A.
Resources	• Estimate 400 to 500 staff hours for actual physician meetings. • Estimate 50 to 75 staff hours for logistical support. • $15,000 for materials, meals, travel mileage, etc.
Responsible	Chief Executive Officer Senior Vice President, Medical Staff Affairs Director, Marketing (Logistical Support and Database Management)

Market Action Example Nine (Uptown University Medical Center)

Action F-3 – Expand Medical Call Center Capabilities To Support Emergency Department

Strategy	*Strategy Two.* Improve consumer access to Uptown services.
Action Description	Expand the medical call center capabilities and responsibility to provide nurse triage support directly to emergency department callers.
	The emergency department currently receives approximately 40 to 50 calls per day requesting medical information and/or triage by phone. This is a distraction to the ED staff. In addition, the ED staff is not equipped to handle these calls in a way that protects the hospital from liability issues. In turn, Uptown does not want to discourage consumers from turning to the organization for help and medical information.
	The recommended solution is to develop a direct connect system from the emergency department to the triage nurses staffing the medical call center.
Implementation Steps	1. Conduct a 30-day evaluation of calls coming to the ED to measure true volume estimates and the types of issues involved in the calls.
	2. Develop protocols between the ED staff and the medical call center staff to determine which calls will be forwarded.
	3. Install phone connection equipment needed to make a direct (no hang-up or redial) connection between the ED and medical call center.
	4. Use the medical call center software to track the numbers, types and disposition of the calls.
	5. Add information to collateral materials, Web page and other sources to encourage callers with medical issue calls to phone the medical call center, not the ED.
Rationale	The ED is currently facing long delays due to increasing volumes and other issues. The reduction of 40 to 50 calls per day would free the equivalent of a 0.5 FTE nurse. In addition, the medical call center is better equipped to handle these calls in a manner that will avoid liability issues and will provide the caller with a satisfactory experience.
Priority	Two
Time Frame	January 200B
Resources	• Estimate 25 to 50 staff hours to establish protocols.
	• No additional call center staff should be required unless call volume exceeds 150% of the projection.
	• $2,000 for telephone connection capabilities.
Responsible	Nursing Director, Emergency Services
	Medical Call Center Manager

Market Action Example Ten (Wolfe Memorial Hospital)

Action 11 – Expand MCO Participation by Wolfe-affiliated Physicians

Strategy	*Strategy Four.* Enhance managed care relations.
Action Description	Ensure that all owned practices participate in and accept patients from all area MCOs (assuming acceptable financial arrangements). (Note: These practices were acquired within the past 90 days.)
	Encourage nonowned practices to expand their scope of MCO participation.
Implementation Steps	1. Determine which plans are not contracted with the owned PCP practices. Determine (via physician input) the reasons for not contracting with specific plans.
	2. Within acceptable financial parameters, pursue contracts on behalf of these practices and ensure openings for new patients from these plans.
	3. Meet with nonowned physicians to determine why they do not participate in specific plans.
	4. Meet with the plans to determine their concerns and interest in additional physicians in the Wolfe PSA.
	5. Encourage physicians to participate in local MCOs. Explore the potential to provide external consulting support to physicians relative to managed care contracts and operations.
Rationale	Although Wolfe is well situated relative to managed care contracts, the medical staff is not. Lack of a physician panel in the PSA will severely limit consumer access to Wolfe Memorial Hospital services.
Priority	One
Time Frame	Initiate contacts by September 200A.
Resources	• Estimate 75 to 100 staff hours.
Responsible	Chief Executive Officer Chairman, Wolfe Memorial Hospital Board

Market Action Example Eleven (Wolfe Memorial Hospital)

Action 4 – Continue and Expand Community Event Participation

Strategy	*Strategy Two.* Increase public visibility of the organization.
Action Description	Continue current schedule of community event participation and sponsorship. Explore opportunities to expand this participation by one or two additional events in 200A. Give priority on new events to the Riverside portion of the SSA. Anticipated events/sponsorships in 200A include: • County Fair (participation) • River Days Festival (participation) • July 4th Parade (participation and sponsorship) • Downtown Art Fair (participation) • Senior Center Health Screenings (twice a year) • Health Fair – River Shopping Center (once a year) • Community College Health Fair (once a year) • Little League, Boys' and Girls' Club, Soccer League, Basketball League (sponsorships) • Chamber of Commerce Fair (participation and sponsorship)
Implementation Steps	1. Finalize schedule of known events and sponsorships for 200A. Secure participation via appropriate registrations. 2. Determine needs for display materials, collateral information materials and promotional giveaways. Order materials in time for event participation. 3. Determine staffing needs for various events. Secure employee volunteers to assist public relations staff-assigned personnel. 4. Develop a list of potential community events in the PSA and the desired portion of the SSA for participation in 200A. 5. Make recommendations to the CEO and secure approval for one or two additional events.
Rationale	As the local acute care provider, highly visible community event participation is essential to demonstrate value to the citizens of the PSA and SSA.
Priority	One
Time Frame	Ongoing, per determined schedule.
Resources	• Estimate 400 to 500 staff hours to plan and staff all projected events. • $6,000 for registration and sponsorship fees. • $26,000 for collateral materials, display materials and promotional giveaways.
Responsible	Director, Public Relations and Marketing Vice President, Patient Services (Health Fairs)

Market Action Example Twelve (Wolfe Memorial Hospital)

Action 1 – Develop and Implement Image Advertising Campaign

Strategy	*Strategy Two.* Increase public visibility of the organization.
Action Description	Develop and implement an image advertising campaign. The focus of the campaign is projected to be on the following: <ul><li>Emergency services</li><li>Obstetrical services (highlighting the new OB practice)</li><li>Facility and clinical testing enhancements</li><li>Specific target on persons commuting from the PSA to the urban core</li></ul>
Implementation Steps	1. Select an external advertising agency via an RFP search. 2. Work with the selected agency to develop the parameters for the campaign—target audiences, messages, appropriate media mix, media schedule, etc. 3. Obtain input from key audiences via interviews and focus groups for campaign design. 4. Develop advertising campaign materials. Review materials with executive leadership and board for approval. 5. Implement campaign.
Rationale	Research shows that top-of-mind awareness and familiarity with Wolfe is below desired levels. Moreover, there is outmigration into the urban core for services that can be provided at Wolfe.
Priority	One
Time Frame	Initiate campaign design by June 200A with launch in September 200A.
Resources	• Estimate 50 to 75 staff hours to work with external agency. • $350,000 for advertising design, creation and media placement.
Responsible	Director, Public Relations and Marketing

Market Action Example Thirteen (Bayshore Hospital)

Action F-2 – Establish Pricing Schedule for Bayshore Wellness Center

Strategy	*Strategy F.* Support the establishment of the Wellness Center.
Action Description	Develop a pricing schedule for the Wellness Center to support pre-opening membership sales efforts.
Implementation Steps	1. Establish needed financial parameters—physical limit for the center, break-even revenue level, market potential for members and target audiences (e.g., Senior Club members, PHO enrollees). 2. Examine pricing systems and levels at competing programs in the Bayshore PSA. 3. Develop a preliminary pricing schedule. 4. Review with the Wellness Center consultant and a cross-section of potential customers. 5. Revise as needed and implement in sales materials and advertising.
Rationale	The sale of memberships to the Wellness Center will require a pricing schedule that ensures both competitiveness and financial viability.
Priority	One
Time Frame	Complete by September 200A in order to allow for production of sales materials 120 days prior to scheduled center opening.
Resources	• Estimate 25 to 50 staff hours.
Responsible	Director, Marketing Vice President, Finance Director, Wellness Center

Market Action Example Fourteen (St. Gerald Medical Center)

Action 34 – Target Families with Children Living at Home (Direct Mail)

Strategy	*Strategy Two.* Provide tactical promotional support to service lines.
Action Description	Develop and implement a multipart direct mail campaign aimed at families with children under age 16 living at home. Target the St. Gerald PSA and SSA plus selected portions of the tertiary service area. Focus messages on the significantly expanded capabilities to generate awareness, familiarity and preference. Include a call to action for a free copy of a newly published parenting guide (with options for different age levels). Estimated target is 26,000 households with children age 16 or younger. Note: This action should be coordinated with all other strategy two actions in support of the pediatric service (component of media advertising campaign, Web page additions, youth group events and sponsorships).
Implementation Steps	1. Work with the external advertising agency to develop the parameters of the direct mail campaign, including number of mailings, messages, and call-to-action logistics. 2. Develop direct mail materials and obtain internal approval. 3. Obtain mailing lists for target geographic area. 4. Establish protocols with the health information line (call center) to handle inquiries and requests for materials. 5. Implement the direct mail effort per the media plan. 6. Track inquiries for materials and requests for physician referral.
Rationale	St. Gerald has recently expanded its pediatric-oriented services via the development of a dedicated 10-bed unit, the opening of a dedicated 24-hour pediatric ER and the recruitment of three pediatric subspecialists.
Priority	One
Time Frame	September, 200A
Resources	• Estimate 25 to 50 staff hours to work with external agency. • $125,000 for design, printing, list, postage and handling. • $15,000 for parenting books (based on a 10% response rate).
Responsible	Assistant Vice President, Communications Director, Maternal/Child Health Services

Market Action Example Fifteen (St. Gerald Medical Center)

Action 42 – Improve Promotional Support for Community Education Classes

Strategy	*Strategy Two.* Provide tactical promotional support to service lines.
Action Description	Provide timely promotion of the community education offerings via the following methodologies: • A "template" print ad, updated every month and placed in the daily newspaper and three local weekly papers. • A listing of all classes, programs and screenings on a special section of the St. Gerald Web page with online registration capabilities added.
Implementation Steps	1. Work with the contracted graphic artist to develop a template design for a community education print ad. 2. Work with the Web page consultant to develop an adjunct page for community education and the ability to take online registration. 3. Update class offerings, programs and screenings on a monthly basis on the St. Gerald Web page. 4. Place updated print ads in the newspapers per the determined media plan. 5. Continue to take class registration calls via the health information line call center.
Rationale	A lack of a timely and consistent communications vehicle has reduced participation levels in the St. Gerald community education programs, classes and screenings. Placement of the class schedule in the quarterly St. Gerald community publication is not timely enough for consumers to make a usage decision.
Priority	One
Time Frame	Initiate new support activities by October 200A.
Resources	• Estimate 25 to 50 staff hours to develop the template ad format. • Estimate 75 to 100 staff hours to work with the external consultant to develop a community education section of the Web page. • Estimate 125 to 150 hours per year to update ad and page contents on a monthly basis. • $2,000 to develop the template ad format. • $4,000 to develop the extension of the Web page to allow for online registration. • $34,000 per year for print ad placements.
Responsible	Assistant Vice President, Communications Director, Community Education

Market Action Example Sixteen (St. Gerald Medical Center)

Action 46 – Explore Retail Sales Kiosks in Owned PCP Sites

Strategy	*Strategy Eight.* Develop alternative sources of revenue for St. Gerald.
Action Description	Investigate the development of or contracting for retail kiosks in PCP practices owned by the St. Gerald Medical Group (31 sites in all). These kiosks would contain health items including vitamins, supplements, books, videotapes and related materials.
Implementation Steps	1. Investigate the specifics of retail efforts by physician practices and other providers via secondary research. 2. Contact retail kiosk vendors for information and proposals. 3. Establish a review/study team consisting of managers and physicians from the medical group. Determine concerns, reservations and other potential hindrances to the effort. 4. Based on all input, make a formal recommendation to the St. Gerald executive leadership. 5. If approved, implement in three to five test sites before groupwide rollout. 6. Monitor operational difficulties, patient satisfaction and profits per site and product.
Rationale	The use of retailing options by healthcare providers is a growing trend. Such efforts, when successful, generate additional revenue via direct cash or credit card payments. Initial indications are that a successful kiosk could generate $3,000 to $5,000 per year or more in profits per site.
Priority	Two
Time Frame	September 200B
Resources	• Estimate 125 to 150 staff hours to investigate options. • Level of investment to add capabilities to be determined.
Responsible	President, St. Gerald Medical Group Vice President, Planning and Marketing

- **Market Action Example Seventeen (Central Valley Cardiology Associates)**

Action 8 – Influence Hospital A's Image Campaign Focus

Strategy	*Strategy Three.* Promote practice capabilities.
Action Description	Influence the structure of the anticipated hospital A image campaign to focus a significant portion of the message on cardiology-related services.
Implementation Steps	1. Meet with the hospital A marketing staff to determine the timing and current scope of the anticipated advertising campaign. 2. (If necessary) Meet with the CEO of hospital A to ensure that cardiology is a significant focus in the anticipated advertising campaign. 3. Provide technical support as requested to the content of the cardiology-oriented advertising materials.
Rationale	As the primary cardiology physician group for hospital A, any positive impact resulting from a cardiology-oriented advertising effort for the hospital will likely also result in a positive impact for the medical group.
Priority	One
Time Frame	January 200A or prior to finalization of hospital A campaign design.
Resources	• Estimate 10 to 15 staff hours.
Responsible	Senior Practice Partners (Drs. Smith and West)

■ Market Action Example Eighteen (Central Valley Cardiology Associates)

Action 11 – Develop Practice Web Site

Strategy	*Strategy Three*. Promote practice capabilities
Action Description	Develop a formal CVCA Web site. While final content of the site needs to be developed, initial content should include the following: • Profiles of the practice physicians • List of practice services • Hours of operation • Maps with office locations • Links to national sources of cardiac-related health information • Monthly cardiac-related health tip from a physician within the practice Once completed, the site should be linked to hospital A's Web page.
Implementation Steps	1. Secure the services of an external expert. (Note: Hospital A has offered the use of its internal expert for a nominal fee via the MSO.) 2. Finalize the initial content of the Web page. 3. Collect the needed information and write the text of appropriate sections (profiles, hours of operation, etc.). 4. Set up the Web page on the server recommended by the external expert. 5. Monitor the number of hits on the page and update information on a monthly basis.
Rationale	CVCA is currently mentioned on hospital A's Web site, but the information provided is minimal. More consumers are searching the Web for health information. Once the initial development costs are incurred, ongoing use of the Web is a relatively low-cost communications method.
Priority	One
Time Frame	Initiate work by March 200A.
Resources	• Estimate 50 to 75 staff hours to set up (working with external support). • Estimate 25 to 50 staff hours per year to maintain. • $3,000 to set up the Web page and to pay for Web site access and support.
Responsible	Executive Director

■ Market Action Example Nineteen (High Plains HMO)

Action D-6 – Conduct Joint Venture Events for Senior Enrollment

Strategy	*Strategy D.* Enrollment and conversion activities.
Action Description	Continue to conduct open house events to attract potential and current members of the High Plains Senior product. Examples of these events include Grandparents Day, Big Band Social and Ice Cream Social. Plan information and enrollment materials will be made available at all events. High Plains will continue its policy of not charging any admission fees for the events.
	Social events will be conducted on a joint venture basis with the Southeast Community PHO, the North River IPA, the Memorial PHO and the Big Bend PHO. Specifics of the joint venture arrangements will be negotiated by the regional provider relations staff, but it is expected that the PHO/IPA partners will provide support equal to 50% of the resources required.
	The target for 200A is four events per subarea (16 events in total).
Implementation Steps	1. Work with the partner PHOs and IPAs to establish a specific list of social enrollment events and target dates.
	2. Determine the parameters of each event (hours, refreshments, entertainment, location, etc.).
	3. Finalize a budget for each event. (Note: Desired support from partners includes facility usage and promotion.)
	4. Promote events via direct mail, local print and partner Web pages.
	5. Conduct events with enrollment materials and representatives on-site.
	6. Follow up by phone with any attendees who indicated interest on the registration cards but did not enroll at the time of the event.
	7. Track the number of participants, number of current enrollees participating and number of new enrollments.
Rationale	Events that attract seniors have historically provided a viable forum to introduce the senior product and to secure enrollment. Over the past three years, High Plains has averaged eight enrollments per event conducted.
Priority	One
Time Frame	Ongoing during the year. Events to be conducted on a quarterly basis unless specific circumstances dictate a more appropriate schedule.
Resources	• Estimate 100 to 150 staff hours to set up and coordinate events.
	• Estimate 400 to 500 staff hours to staff social events.
	• Estimate $48,000 for materials, refreshments, entertainment, promotion, etc. (Note: This represents the High Plains share only.)
Responsible	Director, Senior Product Membership Services
	Regional Provider Relations Representatives (four)

■ IMPLEMENTATION AND MONITORING

■ Okay, The Marketing Plan Is Done. How Do I Keep It on Track?

In the end, the best plan in healthcare is a useless waste of time and paper unless it is actually used, changed, updated and used again. This is frequently the make-or-break point for many healthcare organizations—hence the origin of the term "shelf documents." One of the best measures of the viability of a marketing plan is just how dog-eared the main copies are. If the plan report looks as pristine 12 months from now as the day it came out of the printer, it was probably not a very useful plan.

Having said that, what can you do to make sure that the marketing plan is used and becomes part of the ongoing culture? To some degree, this depends on the style of the organization and the degree of commitment in place from the top down. There are, however, some specific techniques that might help the process:

- *Provide copies to all users.* One way to help ensure that the marketing plan is implemented is to provide full (or edited) copies to all internal parties who have responsibility for implementation. This could also be expanded to include senior managers and department directors who may not be directly involved (such as the human resources VP or the director of housekeeping), as well as key members of the medical staff and members of the board. Encourage all involved parties to read the document and ask questions if any arise.

  There is, of course, a flip side to this open sharing—the risk that the document will get into the hands of the competition. Ideally, you would prefer that your competition not know that you plan to open a diagnostic imaging site in the next county or that you plan to promote your OB capabilities. Clearly, the more hands the plan gets into, the more likely it is to find its way into the wrong hands. There is no easy answer to this dilemma. You need to look closely at the culture of your organization. Is there a history of leaks or of people who move back and forth between competing organizations? Or is the entity fairly close knit and stable?

- *Review the status of the plan every month.* The marketing plan should not sit on a shelf, examined only at the end of the planning or fiscal year. The organization's marketing team (or the managers responsible for the marketing plan) should review the status of the plan on a monthly basis. This includes any significant changes to the market audit information, opportunities for new strategies and the viability of the portfolio of market actions.

- *Send reminders to all responsible parties 30 days prior to startup.* When the plan was completed, the organization had a schedule of when various market actions would be implemented. Staff members within the organization's marketing function are likely to be aware of this schedule and they should be reviewing it on a monthly basis.

Other members of the organization, however (such as the physician director of a satellite office or the director of ER nursing), are not as likely to be paying attention to a marketing plan schedule. Accordingly, these individuals should be sent alert notices 30 days or so before the anticipated startup of the action for which they are responsible. This could be a formal letter or an informal memo or e-mail. A better approach is to meet (again, informally or formally, as appropriate) with the individual(s) to make sure they are aware of the timetable and they have the information, resources and support needed to carry out the market action.

- ***Implement an update/status process from all responsible parties.*** Giving a responsible party pre-start notice helps at one end of the process. Equally important, however, is to keep track of the progress of a specific market action. Again, this need is more acute for situations where the responsible party is not part of the formal marketing function of the organization.

  In most cases, an informal meeting or e-mail may be sufficient. In other cases, a written report may be more appropriate. The methodology used will depend on the culture of the organization, the perceived abilities of the responsible individuals and, candidly, political position. It may be possible to mandate written updates from marketing staff and department directors. It is likely to be a bit more difficult to get written updates from the CEO or the senior partner of the practice of the chief of medicine. What is important is to track progress so market actions don't get quietly derailed while months pass with no progress.

- ***Make the marketing plan a part of the regular business agenda of the organization's leadership.*** Almost every organization has a series of regular general business meetings—the CEO's council of a hospital or the partners' meeting of a medical practice or the management team of an HMO. These meetings usually include some regular agenda items, such as financial status, human resources issues, or the progress of the renovation project. The status of the marketing plan and all related major marketing actions should also be a part of the regular business agenda of the organization's leadership. Giving the results of marketing progress this level of attention will help ensure that plan implementation will become a central part of the organization's efforts and culture over the coming year.

- ***Tie compensation and bonuses to plan achievements.*** More and more healthcare providers are tying the achievement of specific goals and objectives to the compensation structure of their senior staff. Financial performance is the most common factor, but the achievement of specific marketing objectives is also a reasonable measure to use for bonuses, raises and related compensation matters. This is certainly true for personnel with marketing-related functions (such as marketing, planning, sales and public relations). It is also true for other managers who are given total or partial responsibility for one or more market actions. Thus, the vice president of patient services in market action example eleven (see page 81) could be compensated partially on the basis of the successful implementation of the health fair/health screening portions of the community events.

- ***Monitor results on a regular basis and develop a "marketing monitor" report.*** One of the biggest challenges involved in developing the market audit needed to support a marketing plan is finding the necessary data. A great deal of time is often spent during the first round of an organizational marketing plan with data collection, cleanup and interpretation. Unfortunately, many provider organizations allow this database to get outdated until it is time to do the next marketing plan—and then the collection effort starts all over again.

  One way to avoid this problem is to keep the key data elements up to date on a regular basis. Some elements, of course, cannot be tracked monthly or quarterly. These might include the biannual consumer survey or the annual report on HMOs from the state insurance commissioner. Many others, however, can and should be tracked regularly, such as volumes, market share, patient satisfaction, physician activity, enrollment and disenrollment, and contracts signed.

  One way to ensure that data tracking occurs on a regular basis is to create a report that can generically be called the *Marketing Monitor*. This is essentially the marketing equivalent of the financial status reports produced by almost every finance office in the United States. Larger entities with larger staffs and more sophisticated data systems might be able to produce a *Marketing Monitor* report on a monthly basis. For most entities, however, a quarterly report is probably sufficient. A side benefit of a well-done *Marketing Monitor* is that it also serves as the focal point for making sure that marketing issues are on the leadership agenda.

  There is no magic format for a *Marketing Monitor*. An informal document of a few pages is probably sufficient, but the actual style will depend on the resources available and the culture of the organization. While there should be some consistent elements in the *Marketing Monitor*, each issue is likely to contain periodic or one-time items. For example, the following could be the categories for a Bayshore Hospital *Marketing Monitor*:

- Organizational volumes (cases, days, visits, tests, etc.)
- Market share (if the state data allow for quarterly updates)
- Activity by physician
- Gains and losses to the medical staff
- Owned practices and PHO capitated lives
- Patient satisfaction tracking results
- Medical call center activity
- Attendance at Bayshore classes, programs and events
- Web page hits and requests for materials/information
- Status of marketing plan actions
- Press coverage and media expenditures for the past 90 days

Additional categories to be included periodically include the following:
- Biannual physician survey results
- Review of samples from recent competitor ad campaign (with analysis of media expenditures)
- Activities by the local business coalition

- *Be prepared to make changes in the plan.* Take one look at the headlines in the health industry trade journals and it is clear that one of the constants in healthcare management is change—and often very rapid, unexpected change. One of the key axioms of a good marketing plan is flexibility. Market action 12 may have looked good in June, but by January changes in the market have made it obsolete. No problem! Dump action 12 and move on. In June, there was no indication of any opportunity in a community 10 miles west of your location. In October, a developer announces a new subdivision with 2,100 homes. Adding a couple of new market actions (and perhaps a new strategy) may be very appropriate. In June, you thought that action B-6 would cost $11,000. It turns out that it will require $30,000. Budgets being what they are, you may need to drop B-6 or move it back to a second priority.

- *Celebrate success and learn from failures.* If someone has done a good job implementing one of the market actions, give him or her the praise deserved. It may be as simple as a "well-done" note from the CEO, tickets to a ball game or a cover article in the internal newsletter. This is especially true for individuals who are not directly part of the marketing function.

  If the market action does not turn out well, use it as a learning experience rather than an excuse for recrimination or punishment. Marketing plans have learning curves. Organizations and individuals who learn from their mistakes end up with better efforts in the second or even third go-around.

CONCLUSION

One More Time, What Is The Recommended Format For a Marketing Plan?

This is not the only way to format a marketing plan, but it is one that has worked well in a variety of healthcare (and nonhealthcare) settings:

- *Executive summary* is an optional component, based on organizational style. It is best limited to the recommended market position, the list of strategies, the summary table of objectives and the summary table of market actions.

- *Market audit* consists of the analysis of major elements in the marketing environment of the organization along with the key observations resulting from that analysis.

- *Market position* is the "place" in the mind of the consumers that the organization occupies or reasonably can occupy. The desired position is one that is unique in the specific market as well as defensible.

- *Market strategies* are the broad "avenues" the organization will follow in order to secure the desired market position.

- *Market objectives* are the quantifiable targets the organization is hoping to achieve via the marketing actions.

- *Market actions.* The specific activities that the organization will implement in the next 12 to 18 months. Includes a description, major implementation steps, rationale, priority level, time frame, resources required and responsible parties.

What Are The Pitfalls To Watch Out For?

There are any number of reasons why a marketing plan will fail (and conversely, will succeed). Some of the more popular reasons include:

- The marketing plan is not tied to other organizational plans (such as the strategic or facility plan).

- The organization's leadership does not recognize the need for a plan or is just not interested in a formal marketing plan.

- The persons responsible for the implementation of the marketing plan are not involved in the development of the plan.

- The marketing plan is based on poor data or poor interpretation of the data.

- Staff turnover in the marketing function (or other areas) causes a lack of continuity in the planning and implementation efforts.

- The objectives established for the marketing plan are unrealistic.

- The market actions are not technically, physically or legally achievable.

- The resources required to implement the market actions are not available.
- There are no time frames established for the implementation of the market actions.
- There are no established responsibilities for the implementation of specific market actions.
- The marketing plan is never implemented and/or never becomes part of the organizational culture.

■ I've Read The Last 100 Or So Pages. . . . Do You Have Any Closing Comments?

Okay, that wasn't the most creative closing question, but I had to end the book somehow. With luck, this book has provided some insights and direction that will help you develop a marketing plan for your organization. I wish I could create the "template" that was requested during one of my presentations. Simply drop in your data and out pops a position, strategies, actions and so forth. Unfortunately, it just doesn't work that way. There is no substitute for solid analysis of information, the intuition needed to convert observations into positions and strategies, the nerve to shoot for difficult objectives and the creativity to come up with actions that make it all come together. With that, this book will close with these three comments:

- ***Marketing without a plan is possible, but not desirable.*** Clearly, healthcare organizations conduct "marketing" activities every day of the week without formal marketing plans. Quite often, these activities have noticeable degrees of success. More often than not, however, the organization misses key opportunities or wastes resources due to a lack of a flexibly organized approach to marketing efforts.

- ***A plan is not a substitute for action.*** Marketing plans are great tools. They provide a framework for responding to market situations as well as assigning resources and responsibilities. In the end, however, a marketing plan is not a substitute for stepping into the fray and implementing actions that will forward the interests of the organization. Marginal actions based on no planning are still better than a great plan with no implementation. Of course, a great plan with great implementation is the best of all worlds.

- ***Format is not important—content is.*** In closing, this can't be emphasized enough. This book has attempted to outline a format and an approach to developing healthcare marketing plans. This approach works, but so do other approaches. What really counts is the energy, intuition and creativity of the contents.

Good luck with all of your market planning efforts. Feel free to contact me if you have any good stories to tell about successes and failures. This process is part of a never ending journey and I am always willing to learn more.

Appendix A - Examples of Background Data

Introductory Note

The following is a list of the types of background data we would normally request and look at for a typical *acute care hospital marketing plan*. Clearly, the list would be different for a health plan, medical group, IPA or other type of healthcare organization. Once again, the key is to try to look at everything, because you never know where the nuggets will be that will indicate a problem or opportunity that can be addressed by marketing-related solutions.

In all the years I have been involved in developing marketing plans for healthcare entities (or CPA firms or trade associations or any other type of organization), *no one* has had all of the information requested as part of the market audit. In light of this, the market audit process is useful because it stresses the system and shows where the marketing information structure is both weak and strong. It is not unusual for a marketing plan to contain one or two actions related to improvements in marketing databases or information systems based on findings determined during the market audit process.

Organizational Data

- Organizational chart—All owned and sister entities
- Current strategic plan(s)
- Annual reports (past three years)
- Master facility plan
- Current marketing/advertising plans
- Medical staff development plan
- All significant special studies (such as new program potential, patient flow, computer systems, CQI systems) for the past three years
- List of departmental capabilities and services
- List of all off-campus/nonhospital facilities and services

Research

- All consumer-oriented research efforts (past three years)
- Current patient satisfaction tracking results (inpatient, emergency, outpatient surgery and other departments) for the past three years (by periodic measurement periods such as quarters, if possible)
- Medical staff surveys, interviews, and focus group reports (past three years)
- Employee research (past three years)
- Employer/local business research (past three years)
- All other key audience research—quantitative or qualitative

Medical Staff Profile

- Full roster—name, specialty, privilege classification (active, associate, courtesy, etc.), age, office location(s), board certifications
- Analysis of the number of active physicians on staff during the past five years—patterns of gains and losses by clinical area
- Membership (by privilege class) on the medical staffs of competitor hospitals
- Group practice structure—composition of medical groups
- Admission, outpatient surgery and other volume activity by physician (past three years)
- Managed care plan panels on which the physicians participate
- PHO/IPA membership
- Capitated lives assigned
- Referring physician profiles (physicians not on staff at this hospital, but who refer specialty care patients to the hospital and/or its specialty physicians)—name, office locations, specialty, referral volumes (past three years)

Historical Service Volumes

- Historical volumes for the past three years:

    ▷ Inpatient (cases, days) by major service line
    ▷ Surgical volumes—inpatient and outpatient by major service category
    ▷ Emergency services volumes—emergency room, urgent care, emergency room admissions
    ▷ Major ancillary volumes
    ▷ Outpatient and nonhospital volumes—outpatient clinics, urgent care center visits, home health visits

Financial Information

- Audited financial statements for the past three years (to examine margins and overall financial viability)
- Revenues, profit by major service line or operating unit (past three years)
- Payer mix (percent of net revenues) by major service areas and nonhospital entities (past three years)
- (If available) Comparisons of entity pricing versus competitors
- Descriptions of any special pricing packages (e.g., single-price OB for uninsured patients)

Managed Care

- List of local market HMO, PPO, PHO and IPA entities
- Enrollment levels for all local MCO entities
- MCO provider panels—numbers, member names
- Organizational contract status with local MCO entities (have contract, limited contract, no contract)
- Financial arrangement (discount, per diem, per case, capitation) with each local MCO
- Hospital, captive providers or IPA or PHO covered lives (past three years)
- Hospital admissions, ER visits and other utilization statistics by MCO entity (past three years)

Service Area Definition/Demographics

- Patient origin by zip code or county (as appropriate) for inpatient admissions overall and major service lines (OB, medicine, cardiology, oncology and others) for the past three years
- Patient origin for emergency department visits for the past three years
- Patient origin for outpatient surgery for the past three years
- Patient origin for outpatient testing/treatment for the past three years
- Primary and secondary service area demographics (such as current year population, five-year projection, age/sex/ethnic group breakdowns and income levels)
- Employment profile (industry types, major employers by size and location)
- Projected area development, including roads, sewer/water lines and housing developments

Market Share/Market Potential

- Inpatient volumes by zip code in the PSA and SSA (and beyond if appropriate) overall, by major clinical category and by major payer class for the most recent three years
- Organizational and competitor inpatient market shares by zip code, clinical category and payer class for the most recent three years
- Other measures of market share such as public outpatient sources, consumer survey results, share of capitated lives and share of area ER volumes

Competition

- Key competitor profiles for acute care hospitals and nonacute entities (including locations, ownership, capabilities, volumes, medical staff mix and managed care plan participation)

- Samples of recent competitor advertising, press coverage and collaterals
- (If possible) On-site walk-throughs of competitor facilities
- Competitor results from key audience research
- Public information on competitors including:
  ▷ Annual reports
  ▷ Publications
  ▷ State-required filings
  ▷ Recent certificate-of-need and bond filings

Marketing Activities

- *See marketing grid in appendix C.*

Key Audience Input

- Input from a cross-section of key audiences, including internal managers, physicians, board members, area employers, area government leaders, media representatives, and insurance representatives *(See appendix B.)*

Appendix B – Interview Guide Content

What Are the Interview Guides? What Is Their Purpose?

The interview guides are essentially a script used to set the parameters for an input session to support the development of a marketing plan. We use these guides to ensure that we ask relatively consistent questions of all participants. It is important to note that these are only guides, not formal survey instruments. Sometimes a question that is appropriate for one physician (or manager or employer) is not appropriate for another. This could be for political reasons or because it is obvious they know nothing about the specific issue at hand. Sometimes, an interview participant provides an answer that opens up an area of inquiry that was not anticipated in the design of the guide! If so, follow that path wherever it may lead.

The purpose of the interview guides and the interview process as a whole is to provide key audience input to the framework of the market audit. Some issues that might be tested in an interview process include the following:

- *Senior and middle managers.* What is their perception of the image of the organization in the local market (and how does that stack up against the image portrayed by consumer research)?

- *Service line managers.* What is their impression of the support provided by the organization's marketing function?

- *Managers of "sister" entities (such as home health agency, freestanding surgery center, owned medical group).* To what degree do they feel their entity is part of the brand culture of the parent organization?

- *Physicians.* How would they portray the relationship between the medical staff and the management of the organization? How would they portray the relationships within the medical staff (e.g., the usual problems or open warfare between group A and group B)?

- *Board members.* What are the top challenges facing the organization in the upcoming year?

- *Managed care plans.* If they do not contract with the hospital (or the medical group or the home health agency), why not?

- *Area employers.* How often do they have contact with the senior managers of the hospital (outside of occupational health sales efforts and fundraising drives)?

How Many Interviews Should We Do?

Like virtually every other aspect of a marketing plan, there is no magic number of interviews. One parameter to use is that once you begin to hear the same answers consistently from participant to participant you have done enough. On the other hand, if you interview four department chairmen but leave out the fifth one, are you opening up a political can of worms?

Let's use the case studies to suggest some potential levels of interviews.

- *High Plains HMO.* Senior management (5 to 6), provider relations staff (one group interview of 4 to 6), sales staff (8 to 10), hospital/physician/other providers (8 to 10), area employers (12 to 15). Total of 34 to 42 interviews.

- *St. Gerald Medical Center.* Senior management (7 to 8), middle/nurse managers (two group interviews of 6 to 8 each), board members (3 to 4), general employees (two group interviews of 6 to 8 each), physicians (12 to 15), area employers/civic leaders (6 to 7), managed care plans (4 to 5). Total of 36 to 43.

- *Wolfe Memorial Hospital.* Senior management (3 to 4), middle/nurse managers (one group of 6 to 8), board members (2 to 3), general employees (one group interview of 6 to 8), physicians (8 to 10), area employers/civic leaders (4 to 5), managed care plans (2 to 3). Total of 21 to 27.

- *Central Valley Cardiology Associates.* Practice administrator (1), physicians (12), CEO and medical director of primary use hospital (2), managed care plans (2 to 3), referring physicians (8 to 10). Total of 25 to 28.

How Often Do We Do These Interviews and Who Should Do Them?

Ideally, an interview effort of this magnitude should be done as part of the *first* marketing plan for the entity. Much more limited versions of the process (focusing on internal marketing support needs or key hot spots) can then be used in subsequent updates of the plan. The more in-depth and intense process should likely be repeated by the third or fourth update of the plan and then again every three to four years.

Many (but certainly not all) of the questions asked as part of a marketing plan process are similar to the questions that would be asked in a strategic planning effort. In light of this, there is some logic (if the timing is right) in conducting the two interview/input processes at the same time.

Now, who should do the interviews? This is an important question and is usually decided on the basis of expertise, objectivity and cost. Clearly it is much less expensive to use internal resources to conduct the interviews, but it is likely that a fair degree of objectivity will be lost. Will physicians talk about the details of a long-running conflict with management with an internal staff member? Will department directors talk about a lack of marketing tactical support with someone from the marketing function?

Probably, the best approach is to use external support for the first round of the marketing plan, since an error here will be compounded year after year in updates. Internal staff can probably take over the input role in the interim update years, with external support reserved for the major updates at the third or fourth year.

■ Okay, What Do We Ask?

Well, since you brought the topic up, here are some lists of questions that we often use in the marketing plan input process. Some may appear a bit hospital-oriented, but with minimal work they can be adjusted to be appropriate for a medical group, managed care plan, specialty provider or any other health-related organization.

Senior Managers/Middle Managers/Board Members/Physicians

- How would you define the public image of XYZ? If I stopped people on the streets of Anytown, what would they say about XYZ? Are there any services that XYZ is known for?

- What are the strengths of XYZ relative to attracting patient volume (or employer usage or managed care contracts, whatever is appropriate for the organization)?

- What are the weaknesses of XYZ relative to attracting patient volume (or employer usage or managed care contracts, whatever is appropriate for the organization)?

- Who do they perceive to be the major competitors for XYZ (inpatient, emergency and other specific services)? What is the public image of these competitors?

- Are there any significant frictions between the members of the medical staff and the organization's management? Are there any significant frictions between major segments of the medical staff?

- [Physicians] How well does XYZ do in terms of communicating with you about issues that impact your patients and your practice?

- What is the culture of XYZ? What is it like to work here? Has that culture changed in recent years? For the better or for the worse?

- What are the top challenges facing XYZ over the next one or two years? (Could be marketing, governance, finance, facilities or other issues.)

- What are the major hindrances impacting key audience usage of XYZ? What gets in the way of consumers, physicians, referral sources, employers and other audiences?

- Evaluate the effectiveness of the current XYZ marketing efforts, especially in comparison to those used by the known competitors. What works well and does not work well? What are the hindrances to effective marketing of XYZ?

- Within the next 6 to 12 months, what specific marketing tactics would they see as the most needed for XYZ?

- Are there any specific geographic markets that they think XYZ should focus more (or less) attention on?

- What type of key audience image would they want XYZ to project in two to three years?

- [Service Lines/Sister Entities] What are the specific hindrances that your key audiences encounter in terms of trying to use your services?

- [Service Lines/Sister Entities] How well integrated is their service line/entity into the overall system? Are there any significant operational or cultural clashes with the parent?

- [Service Lines/Sister Entities] What are their specific tactical marketing needs for the next 12 months?

Managed Care Plans

- What is their level of enrollment of each MCO in your service area?

- What is their provider contract status with each MCO in the market?

- If a provider contract exists, what is the payment structure (discount, per diem, professional risk, full risk)? Is this their normal payment mode in this market?

- If they do not have a provider contract with any specific MCO, why not?

- Are there any specific services that are carved out from any MCO contracts? Where do those patients go?

- What is the structure of their provider panel (physician, hospital, other) in (area of interest)? Are there any closed portions of the panel?

- Relative to working with their MCO and being attractive to consumers, what are the strengths and weaknesses of XYZ?

- What is the relative price position of XYZ as compared with other providers of similar services in the market?

- How good of a job does XYZ do relative to ongoing working relations with the MCO? What works well and what does not work well?

- Are there any co-marketing opportunities available? Are there any opportunities for co-ventured programs (such as medical call center, health education and screening)?

- [Capitation/Risk Situations] Are there any plan restrictions on actions by XYZ to market to potential enrollees?

Area Employers

- What is the public image of XYZ?

- What are the strengths and weakness of XYZ relative to working with local employers and their employees?

- How good of a job does XYZ do in terms of communicating its services and capabilities to you as an employer? How often do you have contact with a representative of XYZ?

- How important is it to your employees that your insurance plans include XYZ in their panel?

As the reader looks at the list of questions, there is likely to be some reaction along the lines of "they won't answer that" or "their answers will be biased—we can't rely on it." With regard to the first comment, my experience is that the audiences noted above can almost always answer these types of questions. They may choose not to—but they usually can if they want to. As for the second comment, there is no harm in asking a question as long as you are honest in recognizing the potential for bias. This interview input should not be used as a bible, but rather as just one input in an overall audit effort. Internal manager and physician views about the image of the organization should be compared with views offered by consumers. MCO opinions about relative price positions should be compared with actual market data, if available.

Appendix C - The Marketing Activity Grid

What Is the Marketing Activity Grid?

The marketing activity grid is a device that we use as consultants to get a profile of the tactical marketing activities of the organization. This is clearly reinforced with interviews and other data sources, but it provides a quick, clean overview of what the organization is doing.

The example provided in this appendix is one that would be used for a hospital. Some of the elements could be transferred to a grid used for a managed care plan, medical group or other type of entity.

A grid of this type would be useful if you have been called on to develop a marketing plan for a newly acquired entity, where familiarity with the tactical activities used by the entity may not be high. The grid could be completed by the newly acquired entity's staff or (better) can be completed by the person responsible for developing the plan via a personal interview with the appropriate source of information.

The grid could also be useful in evaluating the efforts of your own organization. This may sound odd, but it is not unusual for those of us responsible for the marketing function to lose track of all of the specific activities being performed, especially if the organization is larger and/or has a number of marketing subfunctions.

Organization/Entity Name_____

Marketing Plan 2XXX - 2XXY
Marketing Activity Grid

What are the names of the marketing functions (departments) within the organization?	1_____ 2_____
What is the title of the chief marketing officer?	_____
Who does the marketing function report to (title)? If there are multiple functions, indicate the title of the person to whom each one reports.	1_____ 2_____
What areas of responsibility are included in the marketing function(s)? Please connect each area with the function (1, 2, etc.) noted above. If an area of responsibility does not fall under a marketing function, indicate which department has that responsibility (or none, if appropriate).	Advertising_____ Collaterals/Publications_____ Community Events_____ Customer Satisfaction Tracking_____ Fundraising_____ Government Relations_____ Managed Care Contracting_____ Market Research_____ Planning (Strategic/Facility)_____ Planning (Marketing)_____ Press Relations_____ Sales_____ Other (Specify)_____ Other (Specify)_____

(continued next page)

Including salaries, what is the overall marketing budget for this organization for the most recent fiscal year?

Overall Budget - $_____

Break this budget down as shown.

Salaries/Benefits - $_____

Advertising - $_____

All figures shown at right are:

(Note: Advertising $$ include all media, including direct mail and design, production and placement.)

Centralized in the marketing function _____ or …

Collaterals/Publications - $_____

Other:

Distributed in multiple departments and divisions _____

Promotional Items - $_____

Sponsorships - $_____

Other (Specify)_____

Other (Specify)_____

Indicate the number of FTEs within the marketing function(s). Name the existing positions

Number of FTEs = _____

Positions:

(Example: Publications Assistant)

_____   _____

_____   _____

_____   _____

_____   _____

Indicate the types of key audience research in hand (Include specific audience and methodology—telephone survey, focus groups, etc.). How current is the research?

Audience/Research Type   Month/Year

_____   _____

_____   _____

_____   _____

_____   _____

(continued next page)

Healthcare Marketing Plans That Work / 109

Describe the sales functions that exist within the organization (even if they do not report to the marketing function/department).

List the position, department or program, full- or part-time, services sold (home health, lab services, etc.) and the target audiences (physicians, employers, etc.).

This list should include department or program managers with part-time sales responsibilities.

Position_____ (FT___/PT___)
Dept./Program_____
Service Sold_____
Target Audience_____

Position_____ (FT___/PT___)
Dept./Program_____
Service Sold_____
Target Audience_____

Position_____ (FT___/PT___)
Dept./Program_____
Service Sold_____
Target Audience_____

Position_____ (FT___/PT___)
Dept./Program_____
Service Sold_____
Target Audience_____

Does the organization have an Internet home page or is one being planned?

(If yes, indicate number of hits in the past year and information provided on the page. Also indicate if the page allows for any user interaction (e.g., online patient registration.)

Yes_____ (Own Page)

(Number of Hits/Past Year _____)

Information Provided:

_____   _____

_____   _____

_____   _____

_____   _____

Interactive Capabilities:

_____   _____

_____   _____

Yes_____ (Listed under another page)

No _____

No _____ (Developing one now)

(continued next page)

Describe the telemarketing capabilities of the organization.

If none, check here _____

Not Computer Supported _____
Computer Supported _____

    Internally Managed _____
    Externally Managed _____

    Software/Call Center Vendor_____

Non-RN staffed _____
Mix of RN and Non-RN staff _____
RN Staffed _____

Total Calls Received, Most Recent Year _____

Hours/Days of Operation:
_____

Services Provided:

Physician Referral _____

Class/Screening Information/Registration _____

Health Information (Live) _____

Health Information (Recorded) _____

Capitated/Risk Population PCP Assignment _____

Triage and Service Usage Instructions _____

After-Hours MD Office Triage Coverage _____

MD to MD Consultation Connection _____

MD/Ancillary Services Scheduling _____

Coverage of Information Call to the ER _____

Postdischarge Follow-up Calls (Outbound) _____

Other Outbound Calls (Specify Purpose)
_____

Other (Specify)_____

Other (Specify)_____

(continued next page)

Appendix C - The Marketing Activity Grid

List the names, target audience, frequency and circulation size of the organization's publications (newsletters, magazines, etc.).	Name_____ Audience_____ Frequency_____ Circulation_____ Name_____ Audience_____ Frequency_____ Circulation_____ Name_____ Audience_____ Frequency_____ Circulation_____ Name_____ Audience_____ Frequency_____ Circulation_____ Name_____ Audience_____ Frequency_____ Circulation_____

Indicate the media advertising used over the past 12 months. This should include the media outlet used and the subject of focus of the advertising (organization image, OB, emergency services, cancer screening, etc.).
 	
If available, attach a media plan summary with budget for the past 12 months.
	Print _____
	
	    Focus _____
	
	    Focus _____
	
	Radio _____
	
	    Focus _____
	
	    Focus _____
	
	Television _____
	
	    Focus _____
	
	    Focus _____
	
	Outdoor _____
	
	    Focus _____
	
	    Focus _____

(continued next page)

Media Advertising Used, *(continued)*

     Direct Mail _____

       Focus _____

       Focus _____

     Other (Specify)_____

       Focus _____

     Other (Specify)_____

       Focus _____

List the major public events that the organization sponsored or participated in during the past year (e.g., county fairs, parades, employer-sponsored health fairs, etc.).

    Event _____

    Event _____

    Event _____

    Event _____

    Event _____

    Event _____

    Event _____

    Event _____

    Event _____

    Event _____

Other Marketing Activities

    Speaker's Bureau _____

      Number of Requests/Month _____

    Newcomer Contact Program _____

      Mail _____ Phone _____ Personal Contact _____

    Number of Families Reached/Month _____

(continued next page)

Other Marketing Activities, *(continued)*

Senior Membership Group _____

Number of Members _____

Women's Membership Group _____

Number of Members _____

Other _____

Other _____

Other _____

■ Appendix D - List of Acronyms

CEO	Chief executive officer
CFO	Chief financial officer
CQI	Continuous quality improvement
DRG	Diagnosis-related group
ENT	Ear, nose and throat
ER	Emergency room
FP	Family practice
FTE	Full-time equivalent
HMO	Health maintenance organization
IM	Internal medicine
IPA	Independent practice association
LDR	Labor/delivery/recovery room
MCO	Managed care organization
MRI	Magnetic resonance imaging
MSO	Management services organization
OB	Obstetrics
OB/GYN	Obstetrician/gynecologist
OR	Operating room
OSHA	Occupational Safety and Health Administration
PCP	Primary care physician
PHO	Physician hospital organization
PPO	Preferred provider organization
PSA	Primary service area
RFP	Request for proposal
SSA	Secondary service area
TPA	Third party administrator